The Observers Series
FLAGS

About the Book
National flags are a continuing source of fascination, but also of bewilderment as political changes occur with such speed and frequency in these unstable times. New nations such as Namibia come into existence, others merge or change their regimes. Since the Second World War nearly a hundred new nations have been formed, and since the introduction of *glasnost* important political changes have occurred in Eastern Europe in the last two years. These changes are all reflected in this new edition of this standard popular book. New illustrations have been used throughout with a text which clarifies the complexities of the flags of the modern world.

About the Author
William Crampton is the full-time director of the Flag Institute, the principal documentation, research and advice centre on all matters to do with flags. The Institute is supported by a world-wide network of correspondents who contribute to its resources and enable it to offer information and guidance on flag matters. William Crampton has written numerous books on the subject, including the standard work on the subject *Flags of the World*, published by Frederick Warne in 1981, in which he collaborated with the late Captain E.M.C. Barraclough. He has acted as adviser on several films and has also designed several flags in use today.

The *Observer's* series was launched in 1937 with the publication of *The Observer's Book of Birds*. Today, fifty years later, paperback *Observers* continue to offer practical, useful information on a wide range of subjects, and with every book regularly revised by experts, the facts are right up-to-date. Students, amateur enthusiasts and professional organisations alike will find the latest *Observers* invaluable.

'Thick and glossy, briskly informative' – *The Guardian*

'If you are a serious spotter of any of the things the series deals with, the books must be indispensable' – *The Times Educational Supplement*

OBSERVERS
FLAGS

William G. Crampton

Illustrated by Raymond Turvey

FREDERICK WARNE

FREDERICK WARNE

Published by the Penguin Group
27 Wrights Lane, London W8 5TZ, England
Penguin Books USA Inc., 375 Hudson Street, New York, New York 10014, USA
Penguin Books Australia Ltd, Ringwood, Victoria, Australia
Penguin Books Canada Ltd, 2801 John Street, Markham, Ontario, Canada L3R 1B4
Penguin Books (NZ) Ltd, 182–190 Wairau Road, Auckland 10, New Zealand

Penguin Books Ltd, Registered Offices: Harmondsworth, Middlesex, England

First published 1959
New edition 1979
Reprinted with revisions 1986, 1988, 1991

Copyright © Frederick Warne & Co., 1979, 1986, 1988, 1991
Illustrations copyright © Raymond Turvey, 1991

Originally published as *The Observer's Book of Flags*
in small hardback format.

All rights reserved. Without limiting the rights under copyright
reserved above, no part of this publication may be reproduced stored in
or introduced into a retrieval system, or transmitted in any form or by any means
(electronic, mechanical, photocopying, recording or otherwise), without the
prior written permission of both the copyright owner and the above
publisher of this book

ISBN 0 7232 3699 2

Printed and bound in Great Britain by
William Clowes Limited, Beccles and London

CONTENTS

Preface	7
Introduction	9
The United Kingdom	25
The United States of America	53
A to Z of Nations	72
International Flags	176
Suggestions for further reading	181
Index	183

PREFACE

The serious study of flags is one of the newest pursuits available to those who take an intelligent interest in the world around them. It is a bit like ornithology in that it involves 'spotting', identification, classification, and some knowledge of backgrounds, types, and various features and their functions. It is also a bit like history, in that it includes some understanding of past events and how they came about, and a bit like geography in that the flag student has to know his way around the world (from the depths of an armchair), and to learn the locations of some very obscure places. Its nearest relatives are the collection of stamps and coins, and heraldry. Unlike the devotee of stamps and coins, the flag student does not usually collect actual flags, but only information about them. He relies on books such as this one for facts and illustrations, but he will also be on the alert for flags flying anywhere, particularly in the countries he is interested in. This makes flag study an especially rewarding occupation for those who travel abroad, since strange flags are among the first objects to greet the eye. Like stamp collectors, flag enthusiasts often specialize in themes, such as the flags of football clubs, shipping lines, airlines, cities and regions, rather than trying to take in the entire range of flags of a particular country. They may also specialize in particular periods of history, for instance Napoleonic times, the English Civil Wars, the Second World War. In this way flag students are related to those interested in war games and military modelling, who are also enthusiasts with a keen sense of historical background, and a great deal of information passes backwards and forwards between the two groups. Flags, especially those which are heraldic in origin, or which are complicated and detailed, are also a field of interest for those with artistic inclinations, since they offer many challenging opportunities for painting and drawing.

In a world where international trade and contacts of all kinds are rapidly increasing it is impossible to go for long without a knowledge of the flags of other countries. This knowledge needs to be kept constantly up to date, since national flags can be changed quite frequently, as countries become independent or as their governments change. This can happen in any part of the world, and embarrassing incidents could occur, particularly in diplomatic or commercial circles, if obsolete flags were employed. A handbook of this sort can keep the reader almost up to date, and frequent revisions will help, but it does need to be borne in mind that events can often overtake printing.

Those interested in flags will find that they are among a great many in most advanced countries of the world who have taken up this interest. There are now clubs and societies in most countries of Europe, as well as in the USA and Japan, which are bound together in an international federation. The previous editor of this book, I. O. Evans, was a keen promoter of this activity and did a lot to establish the Flag Institute in Britain, and to make flag study an accepted pursuit with high standards of accuracy and always abreast of current developments. This edition will attempt to keep up to these high standards.

W. G. C.

Note. Figures in the margins refer to colour illustrations.

INTRODUCTION

Flags have played an important part in human life since the beginnings of recorded history. Archaeology has revealed their use in the Iran of five thousand years ago, in Egypt from the First Dynasty, and in ancient China. In these early days 'flags' were solid objects on poles, although often with coloured ribbons attached. The earliest flags of a modern kind were the Roman *vexilla* (from which the name of the science of flags, 'vexillology', is derived), and the *draco* standards. The *vexillum* was a square of cloth hung from a horizontal cross-bar, a form still in use today. The *draco* was a hollow cloth tube in the shape of a dragon, designed to inflate in the wind. This principle was also used in the 'Raven', the standard of the Vikings, whilst the *Labarum*, the later Roman standard, was based on the *vexillum*.

Designs on cloth, usually in the form of inscriptions, came in with the Arab conquests. Designs in the form of heraldic devices developed when the Crusades were launched. In Christian lands crosses were the earliest emblems used by those fighting the tide of Islam, and these came to be worn on surcoats, shields, and eventually on flags. From such simple devices are derived the flags of England, Scotland, Denmark, and medieval France.

Heraldry regularized and codified the growing mass of personal symbolism, and drew up rules for the depiction and use of a coat of arms. One of these uses was on a **banner** consisting of the arms spread over a rectangular cloth. A modern example of such a flag is the armorial banner of the Metropolitan Police. Another way of using the arms was on a **standard**, which came to mean a cloth coloured according to the bearer's livery, and charged with (carrying) one or more of his badges. From a standard of this kind is derived the flag of Wales.

1   A banner of arms: the Metropolitan Police

2   Banner of England

3   Banner of Scotland

4 UK: present royal standard

5 UK: Queen's personal flag

6 HRH Prince Philip, Duke of Edinburgh's standard

Military **colours** are also derived from medieval heraldic standards, but are outside the scope of this book.

Until modern times few flags represented a distinct nation, as opposed to a feudal lordship, a religion, or a military unit. In medieval England it was uncertain for a long time what represented the nation: the royal arms or the cross of St George. But eventually the royal arms came to represent the king alone, and the cross of St George the people and thereby the nation. A similar process took place in Scotland, France, and Denmark. In other parts of Europe city flags, such as those of Hamburg, Genoa and Venice, emerged as the first truly national flags. They had simple designs easily recognizable at sea when used by the merchant ships of these city states. Modern national flags are often a combination of the heraldic and maritime trends.

In modern times colours in themselves, or more usually groups of colours such as red, white, and blue, have taken on a particular political significance. Many countries with flags of two colours, or of three colours (tricolours) have adopted them to signify a political or national affiliation. The flag of the Netherlands was probably the first national flag of this kind, and it was copied with variations by Russia and later by many other countries. Thus the flags of Yugoslavia and Czechoslovakia signify their affiliation to the Pan-Slav movement initiated in Russia. In South America, Argentina and Uruguay share colours which signify their liberation, as do Venezuela, Colombia and Ecuador. In Africa, red, yellow, and green have become known as the Pan-African colours, since so many countries, starting with Ghana in 1957, have adopted them. Elsewhere, black, red, and green, known as the Black Liberation colours, have come into widespread use. In Arab lands red, white, black and green have been almost universally adopted. These colours are thought to signify the whole spirit of modern Arabism. Red flags are now associated with communist countries, but not all communist countries employ them.

KINDS OF FLAGS

Flags have many forms, aside from the heraldic ones mentioned above. Every country has a **national flag**, now seen as the prime expression of national identity, and the supreme mark of independence. The hoisting of a national flag is almost always the symbol of the achievement of independence, a familiar procedure in recent years. Such a flag is for general use by the citizens, although often subject to a code of etiquette. In Britain this flag is the Union Jack, although unlike many countries Britain has never officially adopted a national flag. This shows that a national flag can be established by custom and tradition, as well as by a clause in a written constitution.

Many countries, particularly those in the British Commonwealth, have a distinctive flag for use on civil ships, known as the **civil flag** or **ensign**. This is often a simplified form of the national flag, but in the Commonwealth it is often based on the British merchant marine ensign, the Red Ensign. 16

The flag for use by naval vessels is called simply the **ensign**. In Britain this is the White Ensign, and ensigns based on this are 17 also used in many Commonwealth countries. Others often use an elaborated form of their national flag. Some countries have a distinctive flag for their air forces, known as the **air force ensign**, and even for use at civil air establishments, the **civil air ensign**. Many countries have a special **standard** for their Head of State, and those which are still monarchies have a **royal standard** (or indeed more than one, to cater for the various members of the royal family). Britain is now the only country to employ truly armorial banners for this purpose. Other countries do use heraldic emblems, but often in the form of embellished versions of the national flag or ensign. Such standards were originally and primarily for use afloat, but are now used in a variety of circumstances. One country, Israel, has a special form of the Presidential standard for use afloat.

Finally, one should mention the **jack**, a flag used in the bows of warships (and originally of merchant ships also). In Britain it

7   Prince of Wales' standard

8   HRH Prince Charles: flag for Wales

9   HRH Prince Charles: flag for Scotland

10   HM Queen Elizabeth the Queen Mother

*11 HRH
the Princess Royal*

*12 England:
Cross of St George*

*13 Scotland:
Cross of St Andrew*

14 First Union Jack, 1606

is the Union Jack. Many countries use a flag with historical associations for this purpose, for instance the Irish Green Flag (see p. 120).

WHO USES FLAGS?

This question scarcely needs a reply, since the answer is evident all around us. Certainly national flags are the most obvious, due to the emancipation of so many nations involved in the dismantling of the empires of pre-1914 and the great colonial empires (to say nothing of the dozens of countries which have tried unsuccessfully to secure permanent independence in this century). However, in addition to this, flags are being employed on a wider scale than ever before by groups and institutions of all kinds. One of the most flag conscious countries in the world is Switzerland, and there it will be found that every place, from tiny commune to canton, including every village, town and city, has its own flag. This is also true in West Germany and the Netherlands, and to a lesser extent in many other European countries. Ethnic groups who are trying to establish a national identity also have them, such as the Basques, the Bretons, the Normans, and the Friesians, and many others whose flags can readily be spotted by the alert traveller. There is even a world gypsy flag!

Political parties in many countries have flags, although there is hardly any tradition of party flags in Britain. On the other hand Britain has a great many flags for commercial organizations, shipping and air lines, and for recreational clubs (but not for football clubs, although these too can be found in other countries). Clubs of all kinds, churches, universities, schools, colleges and all kinds of institutions are sporting flags in greater profusion than ever before. In the following pages predominance is given to national flags because space is restricted, and because such flags form the basis of others. But the reader should not feel that the subject has been exhausted with these alone.

FLAG TERMINOLOGY

In illustrations flags are normally shown as flying from the observer's left to his right, a view known as the **obverse**. However, as in heraldry, flags are always described in terms which express the view of the person holding them. Birds and beasts are, or should be, shown with their heads facing the flagstaff side, so that they are advancing, not running away, when a flag is carried along. This side is known as the **hoist**, and is to be understood as the half of the flag nearest the staff. The outer half is the **fly**. A flag is notionally divided into four quarters, called **cantons**, of which the upper hoist canton is known simply as **the canton**. Modern flags usually come from the manufacturer with a **hoist rope** sewn into the **sleeve**. At

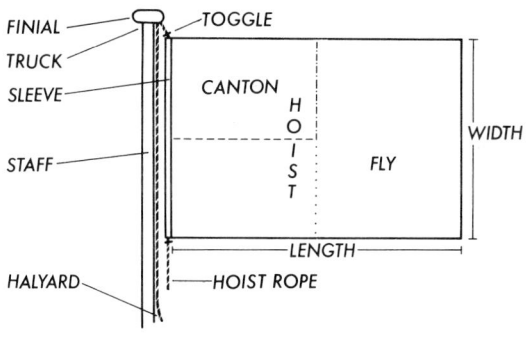

The parts of the flag and the flagstaff

the top of this is a **toggle** which fits into a loop or **becket** in the **halyards**. This tells one instantly if the flag is the right way up, but even so people seem to succeed in getting the Union Jack the wrong way up more often than is statistically probable.

17

15 Present Union Jack

17 The White Ensign

18 The Blue Ensign

19   UK: Chief of Defence Staff

20   UK: Lord High Admiral

21   UK: Army ensign

22   UK: RAF ensign

Modern flags are nearly always rectangular and oblong. Square flags are often found to be armorial banners, and longer flags are usually derived from maritime usage, as with the Union Jack. The oblong clearly preferred by the majority of flag users is the one with a ratio of width to length of 2:3, closely followed by 3:5 and 1:2, although almost every proportion in between can be found. The longest flag in the world is that of Iran, which is officially 1:3, as was that of Poland at one time. This proportion is more suitable, in practical terms, for flags meant to hang vertically, such as are often seen in Germany. Within the oblong shape a number of variations are possible, such as cutting a triangle out of the fly, to make a **swallow-tail**. It is also possible to make a **double swallow-tail** by leaving in a tongue of cloth: a form popular in northern Europe. Flags can also be embellished with fringes, and have accessories such as **cravats** (broad ribbons) attached below the **finial** (the top of the flagstaff, often itself made into an ornamental or symbolic shape).

Triangular shapes are usually reserved for flags of lesser importance than the oblong flag. This is exemplified in naval or other rank flags, where the high officers have oblong flags and the lesser ones triangular flags. Such flags are known as **pennons** or **pendants** regardless of how long they are. They too can be swallow-tailed, a form known in Britain as the **broad pendant**. Long pennons in the national colours were once attached to the lances of cavalry regiments, and still have a number of military functions today. The cravats mentioned above are descendants of the pennons often flown above a flag in bygone days, a practice still followed in the Netherlands, where an orange pennon is frequently added above the national flag. Long pendants are often flown from the mainmast of a warship to show it is in commission, and are therefore known as **commission pendants**. Similar flags can be used on commercial ships and yachts. The triangular flags used on yachts are called **burgees**.

FLAG ETIQUETTE

Care has to be used when displaying flags not to cause offence by disrespectful treatment. A prime rule is that no flag should be hoisted on the same halyard beneath another one: this symbolizes conquest and capture. In fact most of the points of etiquette involve the use of two or more flags together, and anyone proposing to do this is recommended to obtain specialist advice. It is also essential to get a flag the right way up: displayed upside down it signifies surrender, and in some cases it could turn into the flag of another country. It is also considered disrespectful to allow a flag to touch the ground, and lowering colours to the ground is a mark of signal respect to a Head of State. In Britain it has now been established beyond a doubt that the national flag, the Union Jack, may be freely displayed by all citizens, as for example during the 1977 Royal Jubilee. This is not the case with all national flags, however. In many European countries it is considered wrong to leave a flagstaff without a flag, also a sign of surrender! This is avoided by having a long pennant of the national colours hoisted when the flag is not flying. All countries have special days when flags must be flown, especially from public buildings. In Britain a list of days for flying the Union Jack may be obtained from the Department of the Environment, and there is also provision for flying the flags of Scotland and Wales. Flag etiquette is very important at sea, and often has the force of law. Naval vessels, civil ships, and yachts, are all covered in specialized handbooks.

A rule often transgressed by football supporters is that inscriptions or other additions may not be made to the national flag. Flags such as the Red and Blue Ensigns can have badges added, but only by special warrant. At sea, no flag may be displayed which looks like the national colours of any country, and national colours must be displayed when challenged. On the other hand any other flags may be flown in addition, such as a club burgee or owner's (or 'racing') flag.

23 UK: Marshal of the RAF

24 UK: Coast Guard ensign

25 UK: civil air ensign

26 British Broadcasting Corporation

27 British Rail

28 Wales: the Red Dragon

29 Northern Ireland

30 Isle of Man

23

A number of rules exist for achieving reasonable and meaningful designs for flags, and this is also an area where specialist advice is required. Those interested are recommended to contact the Flag Institute in Britain, or a similar organization in their own country.

THE UNITED KINGDOM

ROYAL STANDARDS
The royal standard of the United Kingdom is the armorial banner of the monarch and is inherited with the throne. Its quarters denote the three kingdoms over which the monarch has or has had dominion: England, Scotland, and Ireland. The arms of **England** were adopted in the reign of Richard I, and the Red Lion of **Scotland** appeared in 1165 in the reign of William the Lion. Its unusual border, known as a 'double tressure flory counterflory' and derived from the lilies of France, was added in 1222 during the reign of his son, Alexander II, to mark an association with France (the 'Auld Alliance'). The arms of Ireland derive from a badge known since Tudor times, being based on the famous harp of BrianBorú, first effective king of all Ireland.

The three arms were first 'marshalled' together in 1603 on the accession of James I. At that time they also included the three lilies of France, and these were not omitted until 1802. The present pattern dates from the accession of Queen Victoria in 1837. The banner is usually made in the proportions 1:2 in modern times, due to its prime use as a sea flag, but it was originally more nearly square, or even, in medieval times, twice as broad as long.

Wales was never a united state with arms of its own, and does not figure in the monarch's 'arms of dominion', although there are arms for the Prince of Wales.

The Queen also has a personal standard, somewhat similar to those used in medieval times, distinct from the royal banner. It was adopted in 1960 before her state visit to India and signifies her position as Head of the Commonwealth, rather than as Queen of a particular country. Corresponding royal flags have

31 Jersey

32 Guernsey: flag for use on land

33 Guernsey: flag for use on sea

34 Anguilla

35 Bermuda:
red ensign

36 Cayman Islands:
blue ensign

37 Falkland Islands:
blue ensign

been adopted for use in those Commonwealth countries which are not republics.

6   Prince Philip, Duke of Edinburgh, has a standard, flown everywhere in his presence, except when that of the Queen takes precedence. His standard quarters the arms of the families from which he is descended—the royal families of Denmark and Greece, and the Mountbattens—with the arms of the city of Edinburgh.

7   Prince Charles has three standards: one as Prince of Wales, which is the Royal Standard with a 'label', and an inescutcheon (a small central shield) of the arms of Wales. He also has a
8   personal flag for Wales, which is a square banner of the arms with a green inescutcheon bearing a princely coronet. For
9   Scotland he has another personal flag, with quarters for his Scottish titles. The quarters are: first and fourth, Stewart (for Great Steward of Scotland), second and third, Lord of the Isles; and on an inescutcheon are the arms of Rothesay.

10 The standard of Queen Elizabeth the Queen Mother is an example of an 'impaled' coat of arms of the kind used by the wife of a reigning king. The quarters near the hoist are the royal arms, and those in the fly those of her own family, Bowes-Lyon.

Children of the sovereign use the royal arms with labels like that on the standard of Prince Charles, but with distinguishing marks on the points. Princess Margaret (as daughter of George
11 VI) has a thistle and two roses on her points, and the Princess

HRH Princess Margaret

Royal a red heart and two red crosses. The Duke of Kent, as the grandson of a previous monarch, has a label of five points, and on these three blue anchors and two red crosses.

Although other members of the royal family, such as the Duke of Gloucester, have their own arms, they normally use a special standard consisting of the royal banner with an ermine border all round. H.R.H. the Princess of Wales has a personal coat of arms and a coat of arms used jointly with the Prince of Wales, but as yet has not adopted a personal flag or standard.

NATIONAL FLAGS

The national flag of the United Kingdom, the **Union Jack**, is a combination of emblems representing England, Scotland, and Ireland.

The red cross on white of St George dates back to the Crusades, and has been recorded in use as the national emblem of England since at least 1277. The badge was adopted as that of the premier order of chivalry, the Order of the Garter, in 1348, and came into use as a flag early in the fifteenth century. It was by no means the earliest English flag, and in early times banners of other saints were also displayed. At the Battle of Hastings a dragon standard of the kind described in the Introduction (p. 9) was used by the English, and later taken over by the Normans. But after 1348 other emblems were pushed into the background, and (despite their Welsh connections) a great deal of prominence was given to the Cross of St George by the Tudors, in whose time it was first carried round the world by Drake.

The saltire cross of Scotland has a mythological origin, but is truly associated with St Andrew, who was adopted as Scotland's patron saint at a much earlier date than was St George in England. Like the flag of England, though, that of Scotland gradually evolved over centuries into its present form and colours. When the thrones were united in 1603 a unified national emblem was proposed for British ships, and on 12

38 Gibraltar: the Governor's flag

39 Pitcairn

40 New England flag, c. 1700

41 USA: the Continental Colours

42 USA: the first Stars and Stripes

43 USA: the 'Star-spangled Banner'

44 USA: the present Stars and Stripes

April 1606 the first Union Jack was adopted. This was to be flown at the main top, and the cross of St George or of St Andrew (according to the country of origin) at the fore top. In 1624, however, the Union Jack was reserved for ships in the royal service, and was never again permitted to merchant ships in its plain form. These then began to use red flags with the national cross in the canton, and this was the origin of the modern Red Ensign. From 1707 onwards merchant ships were permitted to wear the Red Ensign with the whole Union Jack in the canton, a practice confirmed in 1864, although by that date the Union Jack had been altered to its present form. This was introduced on 1 January 1801, following the Act of Union with Ireland. The new design incorporated the red saltire cross attributed to St Patrick, for Ireland, in a counterchanged form so as to combine it with the saltire of St Andrew. The shape and form used today evolved at sea in the nineteenth century, and do not conform exactly to the original specifications.

It is now considered pedantic to refer to the national flag as the 'Union Flag', since 'Union Jack' has become so familiar. With regard to flying it the right way up, it is only necessary to note that the broad white band of the cross of St Andrew should be above the red band of the cross of St Patrick in the upper hoist canton. Scouts use the useful mnemonic 'Broad White Top' to remember this. An interesting exercise for budding vexillologists is to count how many Union Jacks are upside down in displays of pageantry.

Despite its lack of official status the Union Jack is now universally used on land as the British national flag. There are no specifications for its use on land, although the Army has adopted its own. It does not have to have any particular proportions or colour shades, and there is no code of protocol for its use. It may only be used at sea, however, in certain specific circumstances, although it has now become customary to paint it on the fuselages of British aircraft.

In 1864 the present system of **ensigns** for use at sea was adopted. The Red Ensign was allocated to the merchant service; the White Ensign, formerly one of three naval ensigns, was reserved for the Royal Navy, and the Blue Ensign was assigned to ships in the government service. The Red and Blue Ensigns could be used, with badges in the fly, by ships of the British colonies, and are still so used by some today (see, for example Bermuda, p. 45). Badges of various branches of government could be added to the Blue Ensign, and with an upright gold anchor in the fly it is also the ensign for the Royal Fleet Auxiliaries.

The correct flag for British registered civilian vessels is the Red Ensign, usually flown at the stern. Certain yacht clubs have the right to fly differenced Red or Blue Ensigns, and one, the Royal Yacht Squadron, may fly the White Ensign. Other flags (club burgees, owner's flags, the flags of shipping lines, etc.) may be flown in subordinate positions.

DEFENCE FORCES

The defence forces are frequent users of flags. Following the creation of the unified Ministry of Defence in 1964 a Joint Services flag was introduced for use at headquarters where all three branches of the services are working together. This is in the blue, red and light blue colours of the three services, with the 'tri-service' badge in the centre. There is also a distinguishing flag for the Chief of the Defence Staff, who is the principal 'unified' commander of the defence forces. This is in the same colours, arranged horizontally, with the Union Jack in the canton and the tri-service badge in the fly. The badge is encircled by the Garter, dating from the appointment of Lord Louis Mountbatten as Chief of Defence Staff in 1965. Other members of the Joint Staff have similar flags which may be flown from their cars or headquarters.

The flag of the **Navy** is the White Ensign (see above). The Union Jack is used as a jack only by vessels of the Royal Navy.

45 USA: President

46 USA: Vice-President

47 USA: Secretary of Defence

47a USA: Chairman of the Joint Chiefs of Staff

48 USA: Secretary of the Navy

48a USA: Secretary of the Army

49 USA: Secretary of the Air Force

50 USA: Commandant of the Marine Corps

Rank flags are used in the Navy and the Royal Air Force. The highest rank in the Navy is the Lord High Admiral, an office now an honorary title of the sovereign. By virtue of it she is entitled to a flag which dates back to the early seventeenth century. An Admiral of the Fleet is entitled to fly the Union Jack, a practice also dating back to the seventeenth century. An Admiral flies the plain cross of St George, the ancient flag of England. A Vice-Admiral adds a red disc to the canton, and a Rear-Admiral another in the lower hoist. A Commodore has a broad pendant of St George with a red disc in the canton. A Commodore on the active list of the Royal Naval Reserve has a broad white pendant with a blue cross. The Commandant-General of the Royal Marines has a blue rank flag with a badge of an anchor and the royal crest, all in yellow. Other officers of the Royal Marines have similar flags. The Sea Cadet Corps uses the Blue Ensign with its badge in the fly.

The **Army** ensign for use on land was introduced in 1938, and has the Army badge in yellow on a red field. Rank flags are not officially assigned to the Army, although many appointments carry distinguishing flags, such as the Chief of the General Staff who flies the Union Jack with the Royal Crest in the centre. The flag of a senior commander in the field is the plain Union Jack. There is also an Army ensign for use on vessels in the Army's service, and there are distinctive additions to the Union Jack for commanding officers afloat.

The **RAF** ensign was introduced in 1920 and is used at all RAF establishments. In the centre of the fly is the RAF roundel adopted during the First World War, which is painted on all RAF planes. A Marshal of the RAF has a distinguishing flag dating from about 1917, with a pattern of red, light blue, and dark blue stripes. The eight senior ranks of the RAF are entitled to similar distinguishing flags, the use of which was regulated in 1938. Since 1942 the Commandant of the RAF Regiment has been permitted to use the flag of an Air-Vice-Marshal (like that of a Marshal but with only one horizontal red stripe) with the regimental badge superimposed. As in the Army there are also flags for the senior commanders, e.g. the Director of the WRAF has a light blue flag with the roundel in the centre, on which is superimposed the 'astral' crown of the RAF.

There are two subsidiary organizations attached to the RAF which have special flags. The Royal Observer Corps uses the RAF Ensign, but with its badge in place of the roundel, as does the Air Training Corps. Ocean Weather Ships come under the control of the Air Force Board, but they too use the naval Blue Ensign with their badge in the fly.

GOVERNMENT AND NATIONAL CORPORATIONS

A very large number of government departments, national boards and corporations, and statutory bodies have adopted flags both for sea and land use. Many departments directly under government control use the Blue Ensign with a distinctive badge. Among these should be mentioned the Customs and Excise and the Coast Guard. The ensign of the Customs service bears the ancient badge of a portcullis that has been in use since the seventeenth century. The Coast Guard badge is a new one, granted on 28 October 1974; before this the service had no flag.

The other British civil flag is the *Civil Air Ensign*, introduced on 23 September 1931, but observed less frequently today than at one time. It is intended to be used at civil airports and terminals and indeed on civil planes if convenient. There is also a Royal Mail Pennant, similar to the one used at sea, for aircraft carrying the Royal Mail, which is often painted on the fuselage of such planes. Some public corporations have distinctive flags, including the *British Broadcasting Corporation* which has an armorial flag featuring the revolving globe seen on our television screens. British Rail has a red flag, often seen flying over stations, with its modern logo in white. The National Bus Company also has a logo flag, of red, white and blue. Regrettably, the Post Office has no proper flag, merely a red sheet with the words "Royal Mail" in gold.

51   USA: 5-star General

52   'Flag of the South'
(the Confederate States)

53   Alabama

54   Alaska

55 Arizona

56 Arkansas

57 California

58 Colorado

The above are only a few of the very many flags in common use, but there are also many regional and civic flags, and a wide variety of public and private organizations making use of flags today.

COUNTRIES OF THE UNITED KINGDOM
Most parts of the United Kingdom have flags for local use, although unless otherwise stated these are not for use at sea, and do not have the status of national flags.

12 **England** The flag of England is the cross of St George, red on a white field. It is traditionally flown on 23 April.

13 **Scotland** The flag of Scotland is the saltire of St Andrew, white on blue, although much use is made of the Red Lion flag, the royal banner of Scotland. Because it is a royal flag the heraldic authorities try to restrain its use by the public—not always successfully, despite a law of 1558 which makes its illegal use punishable by death!

28 **Wales** The flag of Wales is known as the Red Dragon, *Y Ddraig Goch*, and it is now widely used, following its offical approval in 1959.

29 **Northern Ireland** The official flag of Northern Ireland is the Union Jack, but in practice it is only used by loyalists, along with the former banner of arms of the Government of Northern Ireland, which depicted the Red Hand of the O'Neils in the centre of a St George's Cross.

30 **Isle of Man** The flag of the Isle of Man is of ancient origin, and bears the Three Legs of Man emblem which is also the coat of arms. There is also a civil ensign: the Red Ensign with the Three Legs emblem (also known as the *Trinacria*) in the fly.

Jersey The flag of Jersey is said to date back to the fifteenth century. It is white with a red saltire, similar to that attributed to St Patrick, together with a crowned shield of arms, added in 1981. The arms are the same as those of England. The Lieutenant-Governor uses the Union Jack with the shield within a laurel garland in the centre.

Guernsey Guernsey adopted new flags for use on land and at sea in 1985. The flag for use on land is the Cross of St George, as used previously, but with the addition of a golden inner cross, representing Duke William of Normandy, who had such a cross on the flag he used at the Battle of Hastings. In the flag for use at sea, which is the usual British Red Ensign, this cross is used as a badge in the fly. This makes Guernsey the only one of the Channel Islands to have a distinctive flag for use at sea. Three of Guernsey's dependencies also have flags:

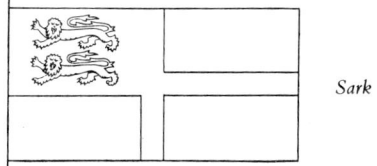

Sark

Sark The flag is a combination of the arms of Normandy with the flag of England.

Alderney The flag is like that of England, with a circular badge of green with a gold lion, placed in the centre of the cross.

Herm A flag was adopted in 1984, also based on the cross of St George. In this case the Arms of Herm, showing three cowled

59   Connecticut

60   Delaware

61   Florida

62   Georgia

63   Hawaii

64 Idaho

65 Illinois

 66 Indiana

67 Iowa

 68 Kansas

monks on a golden diagonal stripe between blue triangles charged with silver dolphins, appear in rectangular form in the canton.

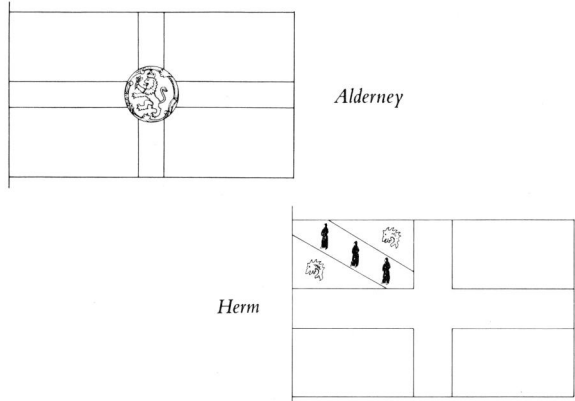

Alderney

Herm

DEPENDENCIES OF THE UNITED KINGDOM

In the following section the date given after each name is the date the territory was permanently acquired by Britain. It is to be noted that those dependencies with more distinctive flags are in looser relationship with Britain than those which merely use ensign badges in the fly of the Blue Ensign. The Governors of colonies and Associated States are entitled to use their badge or arms in the centre of the Union Jack, on a white disc surrounded by a wreath of laurel.

Anguilla (1650)   Formerly a part of St Christopher-Nevis, Anguilla broke away in May 1967. Its position was regularized as a direct dependency of the UK in February 1976. The flag was adopted in October 1967, and a Blue Ensign adopted in 1990.

Bermuda (1609)   This is one of Britain's oldest colonies, and has a shield dating from soon after its establishment, but regularized in 1910. The shield portrays the wreck of the *Sea Venture* in 1609 when Sir George Somers and his settlers first reached Bermuda. In 1915 it was added to the fly of the Red Ensign without any background, and this is now the flag for general use.

British Antarctic Territory (1962)   Formerly part of the Falkland Islands Dependencies this Territory was formed in March 1962. Ships engaged in research work there fly the Blue Ensign with the shield only from the arms, in the fly. The arms are an embellished form of those granted to the Falkland Islands Dependency in 1952. The shield symbolizes research in waters and regions of ice.

British Indian Ocean Territory (1965)   A flag for use by the Commissioner was introduced in 1990, and is used on land only.

British Antarctic Territory: arms   *British Indian Ocean Territory*

British Virgin Islands (1672)   The arms of the Virgin Islands date from 1909, regularized in November 1960. The shield bears a virgin, as in the gospel story, and twelve lamps. The shield alone appears on the fly of the Blue Ensign.

Cayman Islands (1665)   Formerly a dependency of Jamaica

69 Kentucky

70 Louisiana

71 Maine

72 Maryland

73 Massachusetts

74 *Michigan*

75 *Minnesota*

  76 *Mississippi*

77 *Missouri*

British Virgin Islands: ensign badge

the Cayman Islands became a separate colony in August 1962. A coat of arms was granted in May 1958, and this appears on a white disc in the fly of the Blue Ensign. The stars stand for the three main islands.

Falkland Islands (1833)   These islands were first discovered by an Englishman, John Davis, in 1592. His ship, the *Desire*, is portrayed in the coat of arms granted in September 1948, and referred to in the motto. The arms appear on a white disc in the Blue Ensign. The flag of the Governor, now used by the Civil Administrator, is the Union Jack with the Arms of the Falkland Islands on a white disc within a garland of laurel leaves placed in the centre.

Gibraltar

Gibraltar (1713)   Gibraltar has a coat of arms granted by Ferdinand and Isabella in 1502. The arms appear in the fly of the Blue Ensign to form the flag for use at sea, and in circular form in the centre of the Union Jack, within a laurel garland, to form the Governor's flag. On the Blue Ensign the arms include the scroll with the motto *Montis Insignia Calpe* ('The sign of Mount Calpe') and are set on a white disc. There is also a flag for the City, which is a banner of the arms. The use of the arms as a basis for the flags was regularized in 1982.

Hong Kong: ensign badge

Hong Kong (1841)   The Blue Ensign contains the arms granted to the Colony in January 1959. The flag of China can be used on land, and a flag for the Special Region to be formed in 1997, when Hong Kong reverts to China, was introduced in 1990.

Montserrat (1763)   Montserrat became a separate colony in 1962, but has a shield which dates back to at least 1909 when it was part of the Leeward Islands colony. The shield now appears on a white disc on the Blue Ensign.

Montserrat: ensign badge

78 *Montana*

79 *Nebraska*

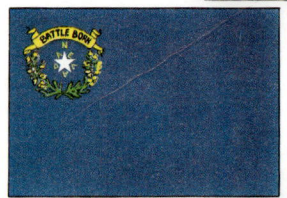

80 *Nevada*

81 *New Hampshire*

82 *New Jersey*

83 New Mexico

84 New York

85 North Carolina

86 North Dakota

39 **Pitcairn** (1887)   A flag for Pitcairn was introduced in 1984, and shows the whole Arms, as granted in 1969, in the fly of a British Blue Ensign. This is for use on land and at sea.

St Helena (1659)   St Helena was acquired by the East India Company in 1659 and became a crown colony in 1854. For many years it used a locally-designed badge on the Blue Ensign, but on 30 January 1984 it was granted a complete coat of arms. The shield from this now appears on the Blue Ensign. Over the scene of an East Indiaman is a yellow chief with a wirebird in natural colours. This ensign is also used by **Ascension Island** and **Tristan da Cunha**.

Turks and Caicos Islands (1672)   These islands were formerly a dependency of Jamaica and became a separate colony in 1962, although linked to the Bahamas until April 1973. A separate coat of arms was granted in September 1965, and the shield from this was placed on the fly of the Blue Ensign in November 1968. It bears a shell, a lobster, and a cactus.

St Helena: arms

Turks and Caicos Islands: arms

THE UNITED STATES OF AMERICA

THE STARS AND STRIPES

The Stars and Stripes, the national flag of the United States, has evolved over a long period since the outbreak of the War of Independence in April 1775. Before this time a flag of nine alternating red and white stripes had been used by a protest movement called the 'Sons of Liberty': the nine stripes standing for the colonies in revolt against the Stamp Act. At Bunker Hill in June 1775 a red flag with a pine tree (also a symbol of liberty) on a white canton was used on the American side, and a pine tree flag was also used on rebel ships later that year. These seem to have developed from a flag used in New England in the early eighteenth century. In December 1775 when Washington mustered the Continental Army at Cambridge, Massachusetts, a flag known as the 'Continental Colours' was hoisted. This was a flag of thirteen red and white stripes, with the British Union Jack in the canton. The thirteen stripes stood for the colonies, and the canton (or 'Union') for the British connection. This was misconstrued, however, as a sign of submission, and so a new canton was eventually inserted, by resolution of the Continental Congress, in June 1777. A canton of stars may have been derived from the flag of Rhode Island, or from already-established military colours, but it is probable that it was the first alternative to suggest itself. Some writers assert that the stars were placed in a pattern like the cross and saltire in the Union Jack, which would reinforce this view.

The Stars and Stripes was intended to have a star and a stripe for each colony. It is now a common belief that the stars were arranged in a circle and that Betsy Ross persuaded the Congress to use a five-pointed star when she made the first flag, but there is no evidence for any of this. In 1795 the number of stars and

87 Ohio

88 Oklahoma

89 Oregon

90 Pennsylvania

91 Rhode Island

92 *South Carolina*

93 *South Dakota*

94 *Tennessee*

95 *Texas*

43 stripes was increased to fifteen, producing a flag known as the 'Star-spangled Banner', as in the American national anthem. But in 1818 the stripes were put back to thirteen, and from then on new states were represented by new stars only, to be added on the 4 July following their admission. The last alteration, to fifty stars, was made on 4 July 1960, following the admission of Hawaii.

44 The national flag is also the civil and naval ensign. The jack is the canton from the national flag.

FLAGS OF THE GOVERNMENT

45 The flag of the President is blue with the Presidential version of the arms in the centre surrounded by a ring of fifty stars, a
46 pattern introduced in 1945. The flag of the Vice-President, as introduced in 1975, has the same arms on a white flag, with four blue stars in the cantons. The four stars denote a member of the Cabinet and are also used on the flags of other members of the government. The arms used on their flags are those on the Great Seal of the United States, as seen in the flag of the Secretary of Defence. The flag of an Ambassador is like this, but with the white disc surrounded by a ring of thirteen stars.

DEFENCE FORCES

47 The Secretary of Defence uses a simplified version of the arms on his flag, in which the eagle grasps three arrows representative of the three services. A similar emblem is used on the flag of the
47a Chairman of the Joint Chiefs of Staff, but the field of his flag is divided diagonally blue over white, with the four stars arranged on an opposite diagonal and counterchanged. The flag of the
48 Secretary of the Navy, the oldest of these flags, is blue with a foul anchor and four stars, whilst that of the Secretary of the
48a Army is red with the whole arms. The flag of the Secretary of
49 the Air Force is light blue with the Air Force arms in the centre.
50 The flag of Commandant of the Marine Corps is red with the Marine Corps badge in the centre.

Rank flags consist of fields in the colour of the service with up to five stars, the highest rank being that of a 5-star General or Fleet Admiral. Officers of the Marine Corps used red flags, and a maroon field is used by the Army Medical Service and a purple one by the Chaplain's Department. Admirals not in command at sea have their stars in blue on a white field.

Each branch of the services also has a ceremonial parade flag. That of the Army commemorates its founding in 1775, and the Navy one uses a seal dating back to 1798. The Marine Corps flag bears the globe and anchor badge with the motto *Semper Fidelis* ('Always Faithful'). The Air Force flag has the same arms as on the Secretary's flag within an arc of thirteen stars.

The Coast Guard also has a ceremonial flag, bearing the US arms in the centre and the name above, with the motto *Semper Paratus* ('Always Ready') and the date, *1790*, when the Coast Guard was founded. There is a special flag for Coast Guard ships, dating from August 1799, with sixteen vertical stripes (this was before it was decided to reduce the number of stripes on the national flag to thirteen), the arms on a white canton, and the badge in the fly. The flag of the Customs Service is like this, but without the badge. The USA also has a special Ensign for Yachts, for specially registered vessels, which is like the national flag but with a foul anchor within a ring of thirteen stars in the canton in place of the fifty stars. This dates from

USA: Coast Guard ensign

96   Utah

97   Vermont

   98   Virginia

99   Washington

100   *West Virginia*

101   *Wisconsin*

102   *Wyoming*

103   *District of Columbia*

1848. The Power Squadron ensign is similar, but with blue vertical stripes, and the emblem in white on a red canton.

FLAGS OF THE CONFEDERATE STATES

52 The 'Flag of the South' is a flag still widely used in those states which were once part of the Confederate States of America, 1861–5. The flag is that adopted as the jack of the Confederate navy in 1863, but it came to be widely regarded as the actual national flag. In square form, with a white border, it was the battle flag of the southern states. The thirteen stars represent the adherents of the Confederacy, not the original thirteen states of the Union. It will be noted that several states which were once part of the Confederacy have flags which are based on the Flag of the South, or on the Stars and Bars, the first true national flag of the South. For this reason the former members are marked (CSA) in the list on pp. 64–5.

FLAGS OF THE STATES

Each state of the Union has its own arms (or seal) and flag. In the following list the date is given of the state's admission to the Union or, in the case of the original thirteen, of its ratification of the Constitution. The second date is that of the adoption of the present design of the state flag. It should be noted, however, that many states had previous designs. The flags of California, Hawaii, and Texas were those of independent nations before they joined the USA.

Many state flags are simply blue fields with the arms or seal in the centre. These often derive from military colours carried in the nineteenth century, or were inspired by the first Centennial in 1876. Some of the flags of red, white, and blue refer not to the Confederacy or the Union but to the French territory of Louisiana, from which several of the states were carved. Flags with red and yellow usually refer to the rule of Spain.

	State	Date of Admission	Present Flag Adopted
53	Alabama (CSA)	14 December 1819	16 February 1895
54	Alaska	3 January 1959	2 May 1927
55	Arizona	14 February 1912	27 February 1927
56	Arkansas (CSA)	15 June 1836	4 April 1924
57	California	9 December 1850	3 February 1911
58	Colorado	1 August 1876	5 June 1911
59	Connecticut	9 January 1788	4 July 1895
60	Delaware	7 December 1787	24 July 1913
61	Florida (CSA)	3 March 1845	6 November 1900
62	Georgia (CSA)	2 January 1788	1 July 1956
63	Hawaii	18 March 1959	20 May 1845
64	Idaho	3 July 1890	12 March 1907
65	Illinois	3 December 1818	1 July 1970
66	Indiana	11 December 1816	31 March 1921
67	Iowa	28 December 1846	29 March 1921
68	Kansas	29 January 1861	30 June 1963
69	Kentucky	1 June 1792	26 March 1918
70	Louisiana (CSA)	30 April 1812	1 July 1912
71	Maine	15 March 1820	24 February 1909
72	Maryland	28 April 1788	9 March 1904
73	Massachusetts	6 February 1788	6 March 1915
74	Michigan	26 March 1837	1 August 1911
75	Minnesota	11 May 1858	19 March 1957
76	Mississippi (CSA)	10 December 1817	7 February 1894
77	Missouri	10 August 1821	22 March 1913
78	Montana	8 November 1889	27 February 1905
79	Nebraska	1 March 1867	2 April 1925
80	Nevada	31 October 1864	26 March 1929
81	New Hampshire	21 June 1788	26 March 1896
82	New Jersey	18 December 1787	26 March 1896
83	New Mexico	6 January 1912	15 March 1925
84	New York	26 July 1788	2 April 1901
85	North Carolina (CSA)	21 November 1789	9 March 1885
86	North Dakota	2 November 1889	3 March 1911
87	Ohio	1 March 1803	9 May 1902
88	Oklahoma	16 November 1907	9 May 1941
89	Oregon	14 February 1859	26 February 1925
90	Pennsylvania	12 December 1787	13 June 1907
91	Rhode Island	29 May 1790	19 May 1897

104 *Micronesia: national flag*

105 *Guam*

106 *Puerto Rico*

107 *Virgin Islands of the USA*

108 Afghanistan: national flag

109 Albania: national flag

110 Algeria: national flag

111 Andorra: national flag

	State	Date of Admission	Present Flag Adopted
92	South Carolina (CSA)	23 May 1788	28 January 1861
93	South Dakota	2 November 1889	11 March 1963
94	Tennessee (CSA)	7 June 1796	17 April 1905
95	Texas (CSA)	29 December 1845	25 January 1839
96	Utah	4 January 1896	11 March 1913
97	Vermont	4 March 1791	1 June 1923
98	Virginia (CSA)	25 June 1788	30 April 1861
99	Washington	11 November 1889	7 June 1923
100	West Virginia	20 June 1863	7 March 1929
101	Wisconsin	29 May 1848	29 April 1913
102	Wyoming	10 July 1890	31 January 1917

District of Columbia This is not a state but a Federal District. It contains the capital, Washington, and it is not
103 surprising that the flag is the banner of arms of George Washington. This was adopted in 1938. The arms are those of the Washington family from Sulgrave Manor, Northamptonshire, England.

DEPENDENCIES OF THE USA

American Samoa The flag was adopted in April 1960. The eagle is for the USA, and it is grasping a staff, called a *fue*, and a club, *uatogi*, Samoan symbols of sovereignty. The field of the flag is dark blue, with a white triangle, fimbriated (bordered in) red. The eagle is in natural colours, and the *fue* and *uatogi* are yellow. The eastern part of Samoa was taken over by the USA in 1900.

American Samoa

American Pacific Dependencies The former Trust Territory of the Pacific Islands now consists of the following states: **Marshall Islands**. Its flag was adopted on 1 May 1979. The field is dark blue with a stripe of white over orange and a gold sun. **Micronesia.** This is a federation of four states of Kosrae, Pohnpei, Truk and Yap, each of which has its own flag. The flag of the federation is blue with four white stars. **North**

Palau

112 Angola: national flag

113 Antigua-Barbuda

114 Argentina national flag and naval ensign

115 Australia: national flag and jack

116 Australia: Queen's personal flag

117   Western Australia

119   Queensland

121   Victoria

118   New South Wales

120   Tasmania

122   South Australia

Marianas. The flag is blue with a grey latte stone surmounted by a white star, and surrounded by a multi-coloured lei (flower-wreath). **Palau.** The flag is blue with a yellow disc and was adopted on 13 June 1980.

Guam Guam was acquired by the USA from Spain in 1898. The flag was adopted in July 1917.

Puerto Rico Originally Spanish, Puerto Rico was acquired in 1899. Its flag dates from the revolutionary movement of 1895. It was made official in July 1952. The design is based on that of Cuba.

Marshall Islands

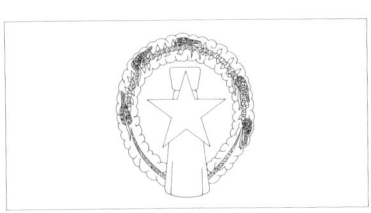

North Marianas Islands

Virgin Islands of the United States   These islands were bought from Denmark in March 1917. A local flag was adopted 107 in May 1921, based on the arms of the USA.

123   Austria: national flag

124   Bahamas: national flag

125   Bahrein: national flag

126   Bangladesh: national flag

127 Barbados: national flag and civil ensign

128a Belgium: civil ensign

128b Belgium: royal standard

129 Belize: national flag

130 Benin: national flag

A TO Z OF NATIONS

108 **Afghanistan** The flag was revised on 30 November 1987 by an alteration to the form of the national emblem. The badge now omits the red star and open book which it previously contained. The central device is a combined pulpit and niche, with a rising sun above and a cog-wheel below, and a wreath of wheat-ears all round. The black, red and green stripes date back to 1929, although they were then placed vertically.

109 **Albania** The national flag was adopted in 1912, but uses an emblem dating back to the Byzantine Empire. The red star was added in 1946, following the formation of the People's Republic. The Albanians call their country *Shqipëria*, the Land of the Eagle.

110 **Algeria** The flag of Algeria was officially adopted when the country became independent in 1962, although it had been used by the liberation movement for some years prior to this.

111 **Andorra** The flag in its present form dates from 1866. The arms do not always appear in the centre, and their quarterings vary somewhat. However, they always represent: Urgel (the mitre and crozier), Foix (three red stripes on yellow), Catalonia (four red stripes on yellow), and Béarn (the two cows). The motto is *Virtus Unita Fortior* ('United Strength is Greater').

112 **Angola** The flag of Angola was adopted when independence was declared in November 1975, and is based on that of the dominant liberation movement, the MPLA.

113 **Antigua-Barbuda** The former Associated State of Antigua became independent under this name on 1 November 1981, but retained the flag and arms adopted in 1967. The flag was

designed by a local art teacher and was the winning entry in a competition. The rising sun on a black field over a blue and white sea represents the dawn of a new era for the inhabitants, whose dynamism is expressed by the red background.

Argentina The flag of Argentina has colours dating from 1810, when independence from Spain was declared. The 'Sun of May' became the symbol of emancipation, and was added to the flag in 1818. The flag for general use does not have the sun. The blue is derived from the blue skies on the day independence was declared, and the sun from its appearance on that day.

Australia The Australian flag was adopted in 1901, shortly after independence was achieved. The design consists of three parts: the Union Jack representing the British connection, the stars of the Southern Cross for Australia itself, and the 'Commonwealth Star', which has seven points, one for each state and one for the dependent territories.

Queen Elizabeth II has a special flag for use in Australia, consisting of a banner of the arms, with the same device as in her other personal standards (see p. 25) in the centre, superimposed on a large golden version of the Commonwealth Star. The civil ensign is the same as the national flag, but with a red field. The naval ensign is also similar, with a white field and the stars in blue. The Governor-General, like those of other Commonwealth countries which are not republics, has a flag of royal blue, with the royal crest in the centre, and beneath this a gold scroll with the name of the country in black letters: in this case, *Commonwealth of Australia.*

Each state has a distinctive form of the Blue Ensign, with its badge in the fly, dating from the time when they were separate colonies. These badges are derived from, or form part of, their coats of arms. The oldest is that of **Western Australia**, dating from 1875 and portraying a black swan. Those of **New South Wales**, **Queensland**, and **Tasmania** were adopted in 1876

73

131 Bhutan: national flag

132 Bolivia: national flag and civil ensign

133 Botswana: national flag

134 Brazil: national flag and civil ensign

135 Brunei

136 Bulgaria:
national flag

137 Burkina
Faso

138 Burma:
national flag

139 Burundi:
national flag

140 Cameroun:
national flag

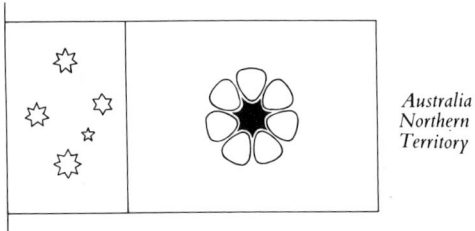

Australia: Northern Territory

and are based on parts of their coats of arms. The badge of
121 **Victoria** dates from 1877, but may be older in origin. That of
122 **South Australia** was not adopted until 1904.

The **Northern Territory** has a very distinctive flag which was adopted on 1 July 1978. The hoist is black, with stars like those of the national flag, and the fly is ochre, with a representation of the desert rose in black and white. There is also a flag for **Norfolk Island**, adopted in 1980. It has three vertical strips of green, white, green, with a green pine tree in the centre. None of the other dependent territories have distinctive flags.

Norfolk Island

Austria The Austrian flag is one of the oldest in continuous use. The red and white stripes are from the arms of the early dukes, dating back to at least 1230, and possibly to the time of Leopold V, who was supposed to have had his white surcoat drenched in blood, except for the part under his sword-belt. The national flag is plain, but the State flag and ensign has the arms over all in the centre. The arms are a black spread eagle with the shield on its breast. In its claws are a hammer and sickle, added in 1921, and on its legs broken chains, symbolizing the liberation of the country in 1945.

Each of the nine states has its own arms and flag.

Bahamas The colours of the flag of the Bahamas, adopted in July 1973, represent the blue seas and golden sands of the islands and the strength of their people. The official specifications require that the blue is of the same aquamarine as the seas around the islands.

Bahrein Bahrein is one of many states in the Persian Gulf with a red and white flag. The serrated white strip was added to make it more distinctive. There is also a flag for the ruler, which adds white borders to the top and bottom edges of the national flag.

Bangladesh The first flag of Bangladesh had a gold map of the country on the red disc, but this was removed in 1972. The green field signifies the fertile land, and the red disc the struggle for freedom. The civil ensign is red with the national flag in the canton. The red disc is not in the exact centre of the flag, but set slightly towards the hoist.

Barbados The flag of Barbados was adopted when the island became independent in 1966. The colours represent the blue seas and the golden sands, and the trident is derived from the former colonial badge. There is a flag for the Governor-General of the same pattern as that for Australia (see p. 73), which is the usual pattern, and also a flag for the Prime Minister.

141 Canada: national flag and civil and naval ensign

142 Canada: Queen's personal flag

143 Alberta

144 British Columbia

145 Manitoba

146 New Brunswick

147 Newfoundland

148 Nova Scotia

149 Ontario

Belgium The Belgian colours first appeared in the Belgian revolt against the Austrians in 1789, and were used again in 1830 when the Belgians campaigned for freedom from the Dutch. The colours are said to derive from the arms of Brabant, a gold lion with red tongue and claws on a black shield, now used as the national arms. The national flag differs from the civil ensign in that the former is almost square and the latter 2:3.

The royal standard is in a dark shade of red with the crowned shield in the centre, and the royal cypher in each corner. The Queen and male members of the royal family have similar flags with their respective initials.

The naval and military ensign is of modern design but uses the saltire, found on local flags since the Middle Ages (Belgium was once part of Burgundy, whose flag was a red 'saltire raguly' on white). The Air Force ensign has the badge of the Air Force in the canton, and the Air Force roundel in the centre.

Flags representing the Walloon and Flemish communities are now widely used in Belgium. The Walloon flag has a red cockerel on a yellow field and the Flemish one a black lion rampant on a yellow field.

Belize Belize became independent on 21 September 1981 and adopted a flag based on the previous unofficial flag for use on land. This was blue with a white disc containing the arms within a laurel garland. The new flag adds a red stripe to the top and bottom, and also uses a slightly revised form of the arms.

Benin The flag dates from 16 November 1959 when the country was known as Dahomey. It was one of many flags in the pan-African colours adopted at that time, but was replaced in November 1975 with a flag of plain green with a red star,

Flemish flag

Walloon flag

and at the same time the name of the country was changed. The original flag was re-adopted on 1 August 1990.

Bhutan Bhutan has a flag with the same sort of dragon as used to appear on the flags of China. The layout of the flag has changed several times in recent years, but the present design was adopted when Bhutan was admitted to the United Nations. The name of the country in its own language is *Druk Yul*, the Land of the Dragon.

Bolivia The national flag achieved its present form in November 1851, although it employs colours used on earlier flags since 1825. The national flag is the plain tricolour, whose colours are taken to represent valour, and the mineral and agricultural wealth of the country. The State flag and President's flag have the national arms in the centre, the main feature of which is the silver mountain of Potosí: the nine stars stand for the provinces.

150 *Prince Edward Island*

151 *Quebec*

152 *Saskatchewan*

153 *North-West Territories*

154 Yukon

155 Cape Verde Islands:
national flag

156 Central Africa:
national flag

157 Chad:
national flag

133 **Botswana** The colours of the flag of Botswana, adopted on achieving independence in September 1966, stand for rain, and for the black and white population. The word for rain is *Pula*, and this is the motto on the coat of arms, which, on a white disc with a black border on a light blue flag, constitutes the President's standard.

134 **Brazil** Many features of the flag of Brazil are derived from those of Portugal, which ruled there until 1822. From then until 1889 Brazil was an independent empire, but when the republic was established the royal arms in the centre of the flag were changed to a celestial sphere. This has twenty-two stars, representing the states, scattered over its surface. They are arranged in the pattern seen in the night sky over Rio de Janeiro. The motto around the equator reads *Ordem E Progresso* ('Order and Progress'). The national flag is also the civil and naval ensign. The jack is dark blue with a cross made of twenty-two stars.

The President's standard is green with the whole arms in the centre. These feature the constellation of the Southern Cross, as in the flag of Australia, within a border of twenty-two stars.

Each federal state has its own arms and flag, some of considerable antiquity. The Federal District, and the capital, Brasilia, each have their own flag, the constitution of Brazil being rather similar to that of the USA. Several of the state flags employ the Southern Cross to symbolize their location in the southern hemisphere.

135 **Brunei** Brunei became fully independent on 1 January 1985 but retained all its flags and emblems. The national flag dates from 1906. The yellow field represents the Sultan, the white stripe the people, and the black one the government. Over-all in the centre are the Arms of the state in red. On the crescent is a motto which means 'Always render service with God's guidance', and on the scroll 'Brunei, Abode of Peace'. The arms were added to the flag in 1959.

Bulgaria The colours date from 1878, when the country achieved independence. The national emblem was placed in the canton in 1947, but it has been modified since then. The present emblem retains the ancient lion rampant, but has it treading on a cogwheel. On the scroll are the dates 681, representing the establishment of the first Bulgar state, and 1944, for the liberation from fascism. This is also the civil ensign. The naval ensign is white with narrow stripes of green and red along the bottom edge and a large red star near the hoist. The jack is red with a large white-bordered red star in the centre.

Burkina Faso The Republic of Upper Volta became Burkina Faso on 4 August 1984 and adopted a new national flag. This is red over green with a yellow star in the centre, thus employing the pan-African colours used by many of its neighbours.

Burma The canton of the flag of Burma was altered in January 1974 from the design adopted on achieving independence in 1948. The present design signifies the union of agriculture and industry, and has a ring of fourteen stars, for the constituent states.

Burma previously had a range of other flags, including a civil ensign of blue over red with the emblem in the canton, and a naval ensign of white with a red cross throughout and the emblem in white on a blue canton, but it is not certain that these are still in use.

Burundi The three stars in the centre of the flag of Burundi symbolize the national motto: Unity, Work, Progress. The flag was originally adopted when Burundi became independent as a kingdom in 1962, but it had a drum and a sorghum plant in the centre. After the republic was established in 1966, these emblems were replaced by the three stars.

Cameroun This country was formerly divided into mandated territories under Britain and France. The French part became independent in 1960 with a plain tricolour in the Pan-

158 Chile: national flag and civil ensign

159 China: national flag

160 Taiwan: national flag

161 Colombia: state flag and ensign

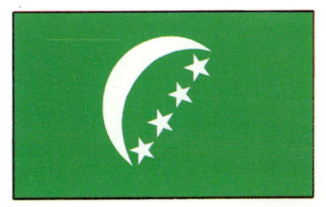

162 Comoro Islands: national flag

163 Congo: national flag

164 Costa Rica: national flag and civil ensign

165 Cuba: national flag and civil and naval ensign

African colours. When the British part joined it in 1961 two gold stars were placed in the canton. In 1975, to symbolize the unity of the country, these were replaced by a single star in the centre.

Canada Canada existed for a long time without a proper national flag. From 1892 the Red Ensign was in use, with the old arms of Canada in the fly, replaced by the new shield in 1921. From then until 1965 this acted as the *de facto* flag, but it was not universally popular, especially among the French-speaking population. Several attempts were made to design a national flag which would suit everybody, but it was not until February 1965 that an acceptable design was adopted. This is based on the popular red maple leaf emblem, and is now the national flag and civil and naval ensign. The jack is a white flag with the national flag in the canton and the naval emblem in the fly in blue. The Queen's flag for Canada is a banner of the arms, with her cypher in the centre on a blue disc within a chaplet of golden roses. The quarters of the arms represent England, Scotland, France, and Ireland, the countries from which most settlers came; in the base is a red maple leaf for Canada itself. The flag of the Governor-General has the crest from the coat of arms on a royal blue field.

Each province and territory of Canada has its own arms and flag. The flag of **Alberta** has its arms on a blue field, and was adopted in 1968. The flag of **British Columbia**, dating from 1960, is a banner of the arms. The flag of **Manitoba** is essentially the British Red Ensign with the shield of the province in the fly; this dates from 1966. The flag of **New Brunswick** is also a banner of its arms, and dates from 1965. The new flag of **Newfoundland** was introduced in 1980 and was designed by a local artist. There is also an unofficial flag of vertical strips of pink, white, green. **Nova Scotia** uses a banner of its arms, which are among the oldest in North America. **Ontario** also uses the Red Ensign, with its shield in the fly. This dates from

1965. **Prince Edward Island** has a banner of its arms, but with a border of the Canadian colours. This was adopted in 1964. **Quebec** has a flag, officially adopted in 1948, known as the *fleurdelysé* flag, which is used throughout the country as a symbol of French separatism. **Saskatchewan** has a flag adopted in 1969 with the shield of arms in the hoist and a prairie lily flower in the fly. The flag of the **North-West Territories** is based on the national flag, in shape although not in colours, and has the shield of arms in the centre. The flag of the **Yukon** is not exactly the same as the national flag in shape, and has the whole arms in the centre. This was adopted in 1968.

150
151
152
153
154

Cape Verde Islands The Cape Verde Islands, formerly a Portuguese colony, became independent in July 1975, and adopted a flag based on that of the liberation movement. This is in the Pan-African colours, and bears a simplified form of the arms in the red strip. These include a black star and a clamshell. The emblem is set slightly above the centre line.

155

Central Africa The flag of this country dates back to 1958 and is a combination of the Pan-African colours and those of France. The gold star represents the hope of African unity. During the period 4 December 1976 to 21 December 1979 the country was an 'Empire' under Jean Bokassa. He had a personal standard of green with a golden eagle, but no change was made to the national emblems, which remain the same as when the country became independent in 1960.

156

Chad The flag of Chad, adopted in 1959, is very similar to that of Andorra, with which it is sometimes confused. The colours are intended to be a compromise between those of France and the African Liberation colours of red, yellow, and green.

157

Chile The flag of Chile was adopted in 1817, although there were earlier designs. It is clearly based on that of the USA,

158

166 Cyprus: national flag

167 Czechoslovakia: national flag

168 Denmark: national flag and civil ensign

169 Faroe Islands

170 Greenland

171   Djibouti: national flag

172   Dominica: national flag

173   Dominican Republic: national flag and civil ensign

174   Ecuador: President, State flag and naval ensign

which provided inspiration for many American countries in their struggle for political emancipation. The President's flag has the whole arms in the centre of the flag. These have a shield of blue over red with a white star, a crest of three feathers in the national colours; the supporters are a deer and a condor; the motto is *Por la Razon o la Fuerza*, which may be translated as 'By Might or by Right'. This does not appear on the President's flag. The jack is blue with a white star in the centre.

159 **China** The flag of the Chinese People's Republic was adopted when the people's republic was formed in October 1949. The Communists always used a red flag, and red is the colour which represented the land of China in previous flags. The large gold star stands for the Common Programme of the Communist Party, and the four smaller ones for the four social classes: workers, peasants, petty bourgeoisie, and 'patriotic capitalists'. This is the only national flag of China, apart from the flags of the People's Liberation Army and the Customs Service.

160 **Taiwan** is the headquarters of the Chinese Nationalist government, which uses flags dating from 1928. Their national flag was previously that of the Nationalist party, the Kuo Min Tang, and was the flag of all China until 1949. The red field stands for China, and the blue canton for the heavens, containing a white sun. There is also a civil ensign consisting of the national flag with four zig-zag horizontal stripes in yellow across the red field. The President's standard is red with the white sun on a blue disc in the centre, and a yellow border on all four sides.

Colombia Colombia is one of three countries which make use of colours introduced in 1806 by Francisco de Miranda: the others are Ecuador and Venezuela. The Colombian flag went
161 through many versions before reaching its present form in 1861. The plain flag is for use on land. At sea a blue oval with a red border and charged with a white star of eight points is added to the centre, to form the civil ensign. The naval ensign

has a white disc with the whole arms in the centre of the flag. The President's flag is similar to this, but with a red border round the disc.

The arms contain a cap of liberty, a pomegranate, and two cornucopiae, and a scene of the isthmus of Panama. The crest is a condor, and the motto is *Libertad y Orden* ('Liberty and Order'). The jack is a blue flag with a white disc containing the arms.

Comoro Islands The Comoro Islands became independent in July 1975, with a new flag based on the red flags traditionally used in the area. The flag was revised again on 1 October 1978, but still has the crescent and four stars of the original design, which it closely resembles. The four stars stand for the four islands, and the crescent for the Islamic religion. 162

Congo Ten years after achieving independence in 1960 Congo transformed itself into a People's Republic, and adopted a red flag with the new national emblem in the canton. This has a crossed hammer and mattock, a wreath of palm leaves, and a large gold star. 163

Costa Rica This is one of five states which were once part of the United Provinces of Central America, and its flag is basically the same as that of the confederation (horizontally blue, white, blue), with an additional red stripe. This design dates from 1848. The State flag has the arms on a white oval near the hoist. These show the isthmus of Costa Rica, and five stars for the five former members of the United Provinces. The flag for general use and civil ensign is without the arms. 164

Cuba The national flag was designed as early as June 1849, but was not established in Cuba until the country became independent in 1902. It is clearly based on that of the USA, but having only one star it is known as *La Estrella Solitaria* ('The Lone Star', like the flag of Texas). Another historical flag, that 165

175 Egypt: national flag and civil ensign

176 El Salvador: State flag

177 Equatorial Guinea: State flag

178 Ethiopia: national flag and civil ensign

179 Fiji: national flag

180 Finland: State flag

181 Åland Islands

182a France: national flag, civil ensign and jack

of the rebellion of 1868, is now the jack. The President's flag is a blue square with the arms surrounded by six white stars. The arms also date from 1849, and portray Cuba as the key to the Gulf of Mexico.

166 **Cyprus**   The flag of Cyprus, adopted when the island became independent in 1960, is deliberately intended to be neutral, in view of the hostility between the Greek and Turkish populations. It shows a map of the island between two olive branches. In practice the flags of Greece and Turkey only are flown in the south and the north of the island. North Cyprus, a state recognized only by Turkey, has its own white flag with a red crescent and star between two red stripes (below).

167 **Czechoslovakia**   The flag of Czechoslovakia dates from 1920, and combines the colours of Bohemia with those of Slovakia, colours which are also expressive of the Pan-Slav liberation movement of the last century. In 1989 a new coat of arms was adopted, which is used on the Presidential flag, and the flags of Bohemia-Moravia (white over red) and of Slovakia (white, blue, red) were revived. Each of these states also has its

North Cyprus

Denmark: royal arms

own coat of arms which are combined to form the national emblem.

Denmark The Danish flag is one of the oldest in continuous use in the world. It is one of the most widely used, loved, and respected in its home land. The plain flag is for general civic use, and the form with a triangle cut out of the fly, known as the *splitflag*, is used as the naval ensign and for all official purposes.

The royal standard is the *splitflag* with a square panel in the centre of the cross, charged with the royal arms. These were remarshalled and simplified on the accession of Queen Margrethe in 1972.

The **Faroe Islands**, a dependency of Denmark, have their own arms and flag. The flag, officially adopted in 1948, is of the same pattern as those of other Scandinavian countries, i.e. with the cross slightly off-centre. The colours combine those of the local arms with those of Denmark.

The flag of **Greenland** was introduced on 21 June 1985. It is in the Danish colours, and represents the sun rising over the ice-covered land.

Djibouti Formerly the Territory of the Afars and Issas, and before that French Somaliland, this state became independent on 27 June 1977. The flag is based on that of the liberation movement, in which blue stands for the Issas, green for the Afars, white for peace, and the star for unity.

Dominica The flag of Dominica was adopted on independence on 3 November 1978 but its details have been altered several times since then. The parrot is taken from the coat of arms granted in July 1961, and is unique to the island. The ten stars stand for the parishes and the three parts of the cross for the Trinity. The stars acquired yellow borders in 1981 and the order of colours of the parts of the cross were also changed. In a

182b French Polynesia

183 Gabon: national flag

184 The Gambia: national flag

185 Germany: the tricolour

186   German Democratic Republic: national flag and civil ensign

187   German Federal Republic: state flag

188   German Federal Republic: President

189   Ghana: national flag

more recent alteration the stance of the parrot has been altered and it now faces the hoist on both sides of the flag. The flag of the President is "scout green" with the whole arms in the centre.

Dominican Republic This country was once part of Haiti, and the liberation movement created its flag by placing a white cross over the then flag of Haiti. Later the quarters were rearranged into the present pattern, and the flag became the national flag in 1844. The State flag has the arms in the centre. The President's flag is white with the State flag in the canton and a large upright yellow anchor in the fly.

Ecuador Like that of Colombia, the flag of Ecuador is based on the colours of Francisco de Miranda, since the country was part of Colombia until 1830. On secession it was decided to keep the same colours so far as possible, so that the national flags of Ecuador and of Colombia are basically the same. The State flag of Ecuador has the arms in the centre, as do the naval ensign and President's flag. The arms show Mount Chimborazo and a steamer on a lake. The crest is a condor, and the shield is surrounded by national flags, an axe and fasces, and a wreath.

All the provinces of Ecuador have their own flags, as do the **Galapagos Islands** whose flag is horizontally green, white, and blue.

Egypt From January 1972 Egypt, Libya, and Syria all used the same basic flag to emphasise their unity. The flag, like the present flag of Egypt, was in the red, white, and black colours associated with Arab nationalism and dating back to the Egyptian revolution of 1952. The central emblem was a golden hawk with a blank shield on its breast, and grasping a scroll with the title of the Federation.

Since then Egypt, Libya and Syria have all revised their flags. The flag of Egypt was altered on 4 October 1984 to incorporate the new version of the national emblem. This is not strictly

Egypt: national emblem

new since it is the one in use prior to 1971. This is an eagle with a shield on its breast in the national colours, and in its claws a scroll with the name 'Arab Republic of Egypt' in Kufi script. On the flag the emblem is all gold, as was the hawk emblem used by the Federation.

The flag of the President has an extra national emblem in gold in the upper hoist canton. The Army ensign has the shield on the central emblem parted vertically red, white, black, and there are two crossed sabres in the canton. The Navy ensign is the same as the national flag, with two crossed white anchors in the canton.

El Salvador The flag of El Salvador is basically that of the former United Provinces of Central America, which was re-adopted in 1912. The civil ensign is distinguished from other similar flags by the motto *Dios Union Libertad* ('God, Union, Liberty') in gold letters on the white stripe. The naval ensign has the arms in full colour in the centre of the white stripe. These are also very similar to those of the United Provinces: the five volcanoes stand for the five original members.

Equatorial Guinea The colours of the national flag, hoisted when independence was achieved in October 1968, represent agricultural resources and the blue sea, with white for peace and red for the struggle for independence. The State flag has the

190   Greece: *national flag*

191   Grenada: *civil ensign*

192   Guatemala: *State flag*

193   Guinea: *national flag*

194 Guinea-Bissau: national flag

195 Guyana: national flag

196 Haiti: State flag and naval ensign

197 Honduras: national flag and civil ensign

arms in the centre of the white stripe. These display a silk cotton tree, and six gold stars for the five islands and the mainland. The motto is *Unidad Paz Justicia* ('Unity, Peace, Justice').

Ethiopia The Ethiopian tricolour dates from the late nineteenth century, and in its plain form has been unaltered throughout the manifold changes that have occurred there. A 178 new national emblem was adopted by the constitution of 12 September 1987, and the proportions of the flag were set at 1:2. The emblem appears over all in the centre of the state flag.

Fiji: Governor-General

179 **Fiji** The flag of Fiji bears the shield from the coat of arms, which dates back to 1908. The shield is quartered by the cross of St George, and is charged with samples of the local vegetation and a flying dove, from the flag of the former kingdom. In chief is an English lion grasping a coconut.

The national flag has a light blue field, the civil ensign a red field, the naval ensign a white field, and the ensign for government vessels a blue one, all following British practice (see p. 33). The flag of the Governor-General is a nearly square blue flag with the royal crest, and the name *Fiji* inscribed on a yellow whale's tooth. These flags all date from the achievement of independence in 1970.

Finland   The blue and white colours of Finland symbolize the blue lakes and white snowfields of the country. The basic design dates back to 1862, long before Finland achieved independence in 1917. The shape of the cross suggests Finland's affiliation to the Scandinavian countries (see also Sweden p. 157).

The State flag has the shield of arms in the centre of the cross. 180 This shield dates from the sixteenth century, and represents the country in arms overcoming enemies from the east. The ensign is like this but is swallow-tailed with a tongue. The President's flag is like the ensign, but with the cross of the Order of Liberty in the canton.

Åland Islands   The flag of these islands, flown only on 181 land, was adopted in 1954. The colours combine those of Finland and Sweden.

France: President

France   The Tricolour as we know it today dates from 1794, 182a although the actual colour combination dates from 1789, soon after the fall of the Bastille, and is thought to consist of the colours of Paris—red and blue—combined with the royal colour—white. The Tricolour was first used at sea in 1790, and revised into its present form four years later. The flag for use at sea has stripes of slightly unequal width. Although the Tricolour

198   Hungary: national flag and civil ensign

198a   Hungary: arms

199   Iceland: national flag and civil ensign

200   India: national flag

201   India: President

202   Indonesia: national flag and civil and naval ensign

203   Indonesia: President

is a simple design, it is so effective that it has proved the inspiration of many other red, white, and blue flags in all parts of the world.

The President's flag is a squarish version of the national flag, with his personal emblem in the centre. In the case of the present President this is a blue and gold tree, half an oak and half an olive, symbolising the unity of France. The Prime Minister uses a square national flag with a heavy gold fringe.

Flags for French overseas territories are gradually being introduced. The first to be adopted is that of French Polynesia, which became official on 23 November 1984.

Gabon The colours of Gabon are another combination of the Pan-African colours with those of France, with which the country is still closely associated. The present design was adopted on independence in August 1960. The President's flag is like the national flag but has the arms in a white disc over all in the centre.

The Gambia The flag of The Gambia represents the river flowing through the green land under the red sunlight, and was adopted on independence in February 1965.

Germany The German tricolour of black, red, yellow, dates from the early nineteenth century, and was re-adopted by both German republics in 1949. The colours are particularly associated with federal unity. They were first adopted in 1848, and again in 1918, only to be abolished by Hitler in 1933.

German Federal Republic The tricolour was re-adopted in May 1949 and has remained in use ever since. In the former German Democratic Republic the national emblem was placed over all in the centre in order to distinguish its version from the one used in the West, which became the flag of united Germany on 3 October 1990. The state flag has the shield of arms over all in the centre: a yellow shield with the black spread eagle which is the ancient emblem of Germany. The naval ensign is like this but swallow-tailed. The President's flag is the same as that used in the 1919–33 period, ie yellow with the black eagle within a red border.

Each of the federal states, including those formerly in East Germany (which were suppressed between 1952 and 1990), has its own arms and flag. Many of these are derived from the formerly independent components of Germany.

Baden-Württemberg The flag is black over yellow, and may have the state arms in the centre. It dates from 29 September 1954.

Bavaria The flag is white over blue, or may be blue and white lozenges. Officially adopted on 14 December 1953, but of medieval origin.

Berlin White with red horizontal stripes along the top and bottom edges, and a black rampant bear near the hoist. Officially adopted 26 May 1954 but of older origin.

Brandenburg The flag is red over white over red in the ratio 2:1:2, and may have the arms in the centre. It was first adopted in this form in 1945.

Bremen Eight horizontal stripes of red and white, with two vertical stripes counterchanged in the hoist. May have the arms on a white panel in the centre. Officially confirmed 21 May 1947, but of medieval origin.

Hamburg Red with a triple towered castle on white in the centre. Of medieval origin, this is a banner of the arms.

Hesse The flag is red over white, and may have the state arms in the centre. Adopted 31 December 1949.

Lower Saxony The same as the German national flag, but with the state arms in the centre on a large shield. Adopted 17 October 1952.

Mecklenburg The colours of blue, yellow, red date back to the nineteenth century. The flag was re-adopted in 1947, and may have the black bull's head emblem on a yellow disc over all in the centre.

North Rhine-Westphalia The flag is red over white

204 Iran: national flag and civil ensign

205 Iraq: national flag

206 Ireland: national flag and civil and naval ensign

207 Ireland: President

208 Israel: national flag

209 Israel: President

210 Italy: national flag

211 Italy: naval ensign

over green, and may have the state arms in the centre. Adopted 10 March 1953.

Rhineland-Palatinate The national tricolour, but with the state arms in the canton. Adopted 15 May 1948.

Saarland The national tricolour, but with the state arms on a large shield in the centre.

Saxony The flag of white over green dates from 1815 and was re-adopted in 1947. It may have the shield of Saxony over all in the centre.

Saxony-Anhalt The colours of yellow and black were adopted in 1947 and may have the shield of Saxony over all in the centre.

Schleswig-Holstein Blue over white over red, and may have the state arms in the centre. Adopted 18 January 1957, but older in origin.

Thuringia The white over red colours date from 1921, when the state was first formed, and were readopted in 1946. The shield of arms usually appears in the centre.

Ghana The flag of Ghana was the first, after that of Ethiopia, to make use of what are known as the Pan-African colours, and was the first to employ a black star—the 'lodestar of African freedom'. This flag was adopted on independence in March 1957. The civil ensign, naval ensign, and air force ensign, all follow the same pattern as their British counterparts.

Greece Greece has been a republic since 1973, and all the former royal emblems and flags have been abolished. At one time Greece had two national flags, one plain blue with a white cross and the other with nine horizontal stripes and the white cross in the canton. The first was used inland, and the other at sea, but from June 1975 to December 1978 the plain cross flag was used as the only national flag. This situation has now been reversed and the striped flag is the only national flag for use on land and at sea, although the plain cross flag may still be seen in unofficial use.

The plain cross flag was first adopted in 1822, and the striped flag about ten years later. Its nine stripes are said to stand for the syllables of the national motto *Eleutheria a Thanatos* ('Liberty or Death'). The President's flag is plain blue with the arms in the centre.

Grenada Adopted on independence in February 1974 the flag of Grenada illustrates the island's principal product, the nutmeg. The seven stars represent the seven parishes of the island. The colours represent sunshine (yellow), agricultural wealth (green), and the friendly spirit of the people (red). The flag for use on land is in the proportions 3:5, and for use at sea 1:2.

Guatemala Guatemala uses the colours of Central America but arranged vertically. This design dates from 1871, following several earlier versions. The plain flag is the national flag and civil ensign. The State flag has the arms in the centre, these consist of a scroll with the original date of independence, and a red and green quetzal bird.

Guinea Guinea adopted the same colours as those of Ghana, on achieving independence in October 1958, but arranged in the same style as in the French tricolour. This pattern was derived from the flag of the dominant political party, which made use of the Pan-African colours.

Guinea-Bissau This country also uses the Pan-African colours, and a black star as in the flag of Ghana. This had been in use since 1961 by the liberation movement. The flag was adopted on independence in September 1973.

Guyana The colours of Guyana are not the Pan-African colours, but represent the green forests, the golden future, and the national spirit (red), perseverance (black), and the country's rivers (white). On land the flag has the proportions 3:5, and at sea 1:2. The flag was adopted on independence in May 1966. The President's flag is a square banner of the arms, which have

212　Ivory Coast: national flag

213　Jamaica: national flag and civil ensign

214　Japan: national flag and civil ensign

215　Japan: Emperor

216　Japan: naval ensign

217 Jordan: national flag

218 Kampuchea (now Cambodia): national flag

219 Kenya: national flag

220 Kiribati: national flag

221 Republic of Korea: national flag

blue wavy lines, a Victoria lily, a pheasant, and a green inescutcheon charged with a crown of feathers.

Haiti The traditional blue and red flag of Haiti was restored on 25 February 1986 after the overthrow of the Duvalier régime. This flag, which dates from the war of independence in 1803, had been replaced in 1964 by the rival black and red version with the strips arranged vertically. The arms in this version were without the Cap of Liberty at the top of the palm-tree, but this has now been restored. The flag with the arms is the 'Official Flag' for use by the President and the Government; without the arms it is for civil use on land and sea.

Honduras The flag of Honduras is very similar to that of the United Provinces of Central America. The five stars represent the five original members. The flag with stars is the national flag and civil ensign. The State flag and naval ensign has the national emblem in the centre. This consists of a pyramid rising from the sea within an oval with the legend *Libre Soberana Independiente* ('Free, Sovereign, Independent'); this is surrounded by two cornucopiae and a landscape strewn with allegorical items.

Hungary The colours of Hungary are based on those of the ancient coat of arms. The flag came into use in 1848, and over the years the state flag has had various emblems in the centre, including Communist ones in the period 1947–56. The flag for civil use is without the arms, which were restored in their ancient form on 3 July 1990.

Iceland The colours of Iceland are a combination of those of its old coat of arms and those of Denmark, and are also those of Norway. The flag dates from 1913 and was officially established in 1918. It became that of the independent republic in June 1944. The naval ensign is like the national flag, but with a swallow-tail. The President's flag is like the ensign, but with a white panel in the centre of the cross, bearing the coat of arms. The shield dates from 1919, but is now supported by creatures from ancient Norse myth.

India The flag of India was originally that of the Indian National Congress, with a blue Buddhist emblem, known as the *chakra*, added on independence in August 1947. The colours represent renunciation, peace and Nature. The civil ensign and naval ensign are of the same pattern as those of the UK (see p. 33).

The President's flag is quartered blue and red, charged with the state emblem in the first quarter, the Lions of Asoka; then an elephant outlined in yellow, a pair of scales, and a bowl of lotus blossoms.

Indonesia The colours of Indonesia date back to the medieval empire that flourished in this area. The flag was introduced in 1945 and became that of the independent republic in December 1949. The jack is the flag of the pre-war independence movement. The President's flag is in yellow (the 'royal' colour), and is charged with a gold star within a wreath of rice and cotton.

Iran The flag of Iran developed slowly over several centuries, and for over a century bore the well-known lion and sun emblem. The tricolour form was adopted in 1907, and was at first very long and with unusual shades of colour. In April 1980 Iran became an Islamic Republic, and a new version of the national flag was adopted, containing the new national emblem in red in the centre, in place of the crowned lion and sun. It also has the inscription *Allah Akbar* repeated 22 times along the edges of the red and green stripes. This symbolises the date *22 Bahman 1358* (=11 February 1979) when the Ayatollah Khomeini returned to Iran.

Iraq The present national flag dates from 1963, and is based on that of the former United Arab Republic. The three stars stand for the union it was intended to effect with Egypt and Syria. The colours are those of the Arab liberation movement (see p. 12).

222 Korean People's Democratic Republic: national flag

223 Kuwait: national flag

224 Laos: national flag

225 Lebanon: national flag

226 Lesotho: national flag

227 Liberia: national flag and civil ensign

228 Libya: national flag

229 Liechtenstein: national flag

230 Luxembourg: national flag

119

206 **Ireland** The Irish Tricolour dates from 1848. The colours symbolize the Protestants (orange) and the Catholics (green), and the peace resulting from a united Ireland. It was adopted by the Irish Free State in 1920.

207 The President's flag features the ancient harp of Brian Boru, which is also found in British royal heraldry. The jack is green, with the same harp in yellow. This flag ('The Green Flag'), was the earliest symbol of the Home Rule movement.

208 **Israel** The flag of Israel dates back to the earliest days of Zionism. Its central emblem is the *Magen David* ('Shield of David'), and the blue and white stripes are taken from the Hebrew *tallith*, or prayer-shawl. It was adopted when Israel became independent in May 1948. The civil ensign is also blue,
209 with the *Magen David* on a white oval. The President's flag is a banner of the arms, which employ the *menorah*, the seven-branched candlestick which once stood in the Temple of Jerusalem. Around this is a wreath of olive, and underneath the name 'Israel' in Hebrew.

210 **Italy** The Italian Tricolour has its origin in Napoleon's liberation of the 1790s, and it is probable that the design is based on that of France. The flag did not become permanent until 1848, and did not become that of a united Italy until 1861.

In 1946 the arms of Savoy were removed from the centre, and the flag is now quite plain. New civil and naval ensigns were introduced at that time, with a new shield in the centre.
211 The shield contains the arms of Venice, Genoa, Amalfi, and Pisa, but the quarter for Venice is slightly different in the naval ensign from that in the civil ensign. The jack is a banner of the arms as in the naval ensign.

212 **Ivory Coast (Côte d'Ivoire)** The flag was introduced in 1959, and is probably based on that of France. A variety of meanings are attached to the colours.

Jamaica The flag was adopted on independence in August 213
1962. The colours stand for the agricultural and mineral wealth
of the island and the hardships facing its people. The royal flag
is a banner of the arms with the royal cypher in the centre. The
naval ensign is like that of Britain (p. 33), with the national flag
in the canton. The Governor-General's flag is royal blue with
the royal crest and the name *Jamaica* on a gold scroll.

Japan The red sun on the flag of Japan represents the 'land of 214
the rising sun', and is known as a *mon*, a purely Japanese heraldic
form. The chrysanthemum on the royal standard is also a *mon*, 215
and forms the national emblem. The naval ensign is the same as 216
that used before the Second World War, and was restored to
use in 1954.

Jordan The flag of Jordan is derived from that used in the
first Arab revolt of 1917 and the colours are known as the Pan- 217
Arab colours (see p. 12). The seven-pointed star was added to
distinguish the flag from that then used in the Hedjaz, and its
points stand for the basic tenets of the Moslem faith. Without
the star this flag is used by the protagonists of Arab Palestine.

The naval ensign is white with the national flag in the canton
and the combined services emblem in the fly in black. The
royal standard is a complicated flag of pieces in the Arab colours
and the national flag in the centre, but with a crown in place of
the star.

Kampuchea (Cambodia) The regime in control of Phnom
Penh introduced a new version of the national flag on 1 May 218
1989, in which the temple appears in full detail in yellow on a
field of red and blue. The rival regime has a flag of blue, red,
blue with the temple in white in the centre of the red stripe,
which is twice the width of the others.

Kenya Introduced when Kenya became independent in 219
December 1963, the colours of the flag are based on those of the
dominant political party, and are also those of the 'Black

231   *Madagascar: national flag*

232   *Malawi: national flag*

233   *Malaysia: national flag and civil ensign*

234   *Maldive Islands: national flag*

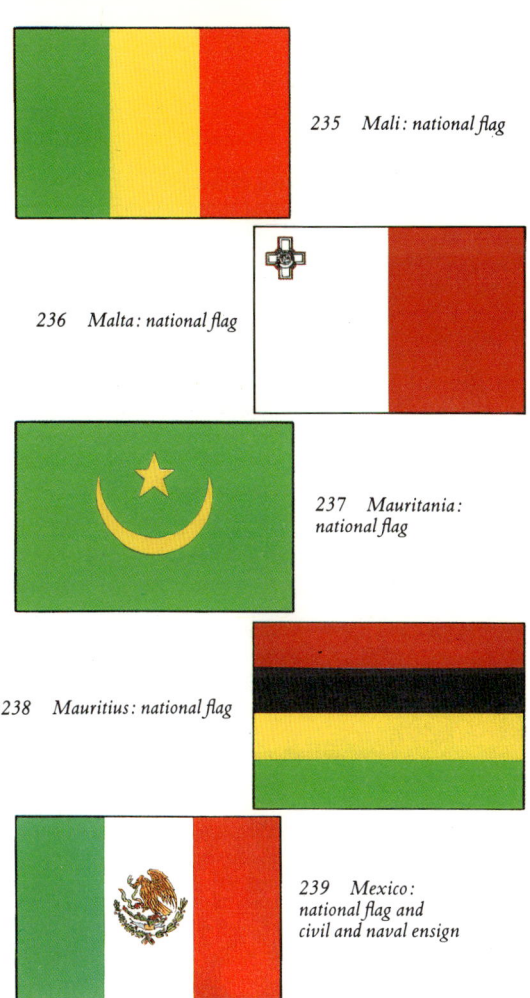

235   Mali: national flag

236   Malta: national flag

237   Mauritania: national flag

238   Mauritius: national flag

239   Mexico: national flag and civil and naval ensign

Liberation' movement. The red in this case is a special shade known as 'Kenya red'. The naval ensign is white with the national flag in the canton and a red vertical anchor in the fly.

Kiribati The former Gilbert Islands became independent under this name in July 1979, and adopted a flag based on the coat of arms. The coat of arms of the then Gilbert and Ellice Islands was granted in 1937, and the shield was used as an ensign badge until the independence of the Gilbert Islands. The Ellice Islands, now known as Tuvalu, became a separate colony in 1975.

Korea, Republic of The strange devices on the flag of South Korea are: in the centre the *yang-yin* and around it four *kwae* symbols. The first represents the union of opposites, and the latter the four seasons, the four winds, etc. This flag was adopted in January 1950, but is based on that used by Korea before 1910.

Korean People's Democratic Republic This flag was adopted in September 1948 for the republic formed at that time in North Korea. The colours are the same as those of the original Korean flag but in a new Communist pattern.

Kuwait A new flag was adopted by Kuwait when independence was achieved in November 1961. The colours are the Pan-Arab colours (p. 12).

Laos Laos became a Communist republic in December 1975, and the flag of the Pathet Lao was adopted. The blue stripe is said to represent the Mekong River, the disc the moon, and the red the unity of purpose of the Laos and the Vietnamese.

Lebanon The cedar tree has been the symbol of the Lebanon since Biblical times. It was placed on the present flag in December 1943 when the country became independent. The red and white colours are probably derived from those of the Lebanese Legion in the First World War.

Lesotho The present flag of Lesotho was adopted on 20 January 1987 and replaced the one hoisted when the country became independent. In the white section is an outline of the shield and weapons from the national arms. The arms appear in full colour in this position on the Royal Standard.

Liberia The flag of Liberia is clearly based on that of the USA, from whence most of its immigrants came, except that it has only eleven stripes and one white star. It was adopted on independence in July 1847. The largest single number of merchant ships in the world sail under this flag.

The flag of the President is square and blue with the stripes from the national flag arranged vertically on a shield with a blue chief with one white star and a gold border. In each canton is a white star. The jack is blue with a single white star.

Libya: national emblem

Libya Libya was a founder-member of the Federation of Arab Republics in 1972, but broke away in 1977 when Egypt began peace negotiations with Israel. From then on a plain green flag has been in use, symbolising the 'Green Revolution'. The national emblem has been altered to include a green shield on the falcon's breast and the title 'Libyan Arab Republic' on the scroll.

Liechtenstein The colours of Liechtenstein date back to the early nineteenth century. The coronet was added in 1937 to avoid confusion with the then flag of Haiti. The Prince's flag is

240   Monaco: national flag

241   Mongolia: national flag

242   Morocco: national flag

243   Mozambique:
national flag

243a   Namibia: national flag

244 Nauru: national flag

245 Nepal: national flag

246 Netherlands: national flag and civil and naval ensign

247 Netherlands: jack

248 Netherlands: royal standard

blue over red with the whole arms over all in the centre and a yellow border all round. The state flag is like this but without the yellow border.

Luxembourg The colours of Luxembourg are derived from the coat of arms, which is like the civil ensign, having blue and white stripes with a red lion rampant over all. The blue is usually a shade lighter than in the flag of the Netherlands. The national flag can further be distinguished from that of the Netherlands by its ratio, which is 3:5 rather than 2:3.

The present standard of the Grand Duke was adopted soon after his accession in 1964. It has a blue field with golden billets, from the arms of the House of Orange-Nassau, and the shield of Luxembourg within the collar of the Order of the Oaken Crown.

Madagascar When Madagascar was an independent kingdom its flags were all red and white. Green was added when the republic was formed in 1958. Red and white are said to stand for the Hova people, and green for the coastal inhabitants.

Malawi The flag of Malawi was adopted on independence in July 1964, on the basis of the flag of the dominant political party, and uses the Black Liberation colours (see Kenya p. 121). The red sun is from the old arms of Nyasaland. The President's flag is red with the gold lion passant from the arms, and a scroll with the name *Malawi* in black letters.

Malaysia The stripes of the national flag stand for the members of the federation and for the Federal District, as do the points of the star in the canton. The flag was adopted in September 1963 on the basis of that of Malaya. The civil ensign is red with the national flag fimbriated blue (i.e. with a blue border) in the canton. The naval ensign is white with the national flag in the canton and the combined services emblem in the fly in blue.

All the states of Malaysia have their own arms and flags.

Maldive Islands The flag of the Maldives has evolved over a number of years from a plain red one. The present design was adopted in July 1965. The flag of the Head of State has a crescent as well as a star in the centre.

Mali The colours of Mali are the Pan-African colours arranged in the same form as the French Tricolour. The flag was adopted when the country became independent in September 1960.

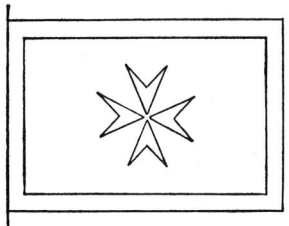

Malta: civil ensign

Malta The flag of Malta is of considerable antiquity, being derived from the colours of the arms of the Knights of St John. The cross of the George Cross was added in 1943 on a small blue canton, which was removed on independence in September 1964. The well-known badge of the Maltese Cross appears on the civil ensign and on the President's flag which was introduced with a new version of the arms on 28 October 1988.

Mauritania The flag of Mauritania was adopted in April 1959 and the Moslem star and crescent moon express the country's official title: the Islamic Republic of Mauritania.

Mauritius The colours of the flag are derived from the coat of arms, but are capable of several interpretations. The flag was adopted on independence in March 1968. The civil ensign is red with the national flag in the canton and the arms on a white disc in the fly.

249 Netherlands Antilles

250 Aruba

251 Bonaire

252 Curacao

253 New Zealand: national flag and jack

254 New Zealand: Queen's personal flag

255 Cook Islands

256 Niue

257 Nicaragua: national flag and civil and naval ensign

239 **Mexico** The emblem on the flag of Mexico is the old Aztec symbol for Mexico City, formerly Tenochtitlán, where, according to legend, the wandering Aztecs found an eagle grasping a snake whilst standing on a cactus on an island in the middle of a lake. The colours of the flag derive from a flag used in the independence movement of the 1820s, standing for independence, unity, and religion. The central emblem has varied over the years: the present form was established in September 1968. The same flag serves as President's standard, national flag, and civil and naval ensign.

240 **Monaco** The colours of the flag are derived from the arms of the principality, which are of medieval origin. The present form of the flag was adopted in 1881. The Prince's standard is white with the whole arms in the centre. The national flag may be distinguished from that of Indonesia by its ratio—4:5 compared with 2:3.

241 **Mongolia** The blue in the flag of Mongolia is the particular colour of the Mongols, whilst red stands for revolution. The emblem in the hoist is the *soyonbo*, a combination of various abstract devices surmounted by the gold star of communism. The present design was adopted in February 1949.

242 **Morocco** The flag of Morocco dates from 1915, when the green pentacle, or 'Solomon's Seal', was added to the previously plain red flag. Morocco regained its independence in 1956 and retained the already-established flag. The naval ensign adds the royal crown in gold in the canton.

243 **Mozambique** A new design for the national flag was adopted in April 1983, which reverts to the form of the flag of the liberation movement Frelimo and replaces the flag adopted on independence in 1975. In the red triangle is a gold star charted with a crossed rifle and mattock surmounting an open book. These elements are taken from the national emblem.

Namibia   The former Trust Territory of South-West Africa became independent on 21 March 1990. The flag hoisted then is based on the colours of SWAPO, the main liberation movement, together with those of the opposition parties. In the canton is a sun like that in the flag of Taiwan, said to represent the twelve main ethnic groups. There is also a new coat of arms, based on the flag design.

Nauru   This island lies just south of the Equator, as expressed by the design of its flag. The star represents the island, and the twelve points its twelve native tribes. The flag was adopted on independence in January 1968.

Nepal   This is the only national flag that is not rectangular. The design was streamlined in December 1962 but still retains the emblems of the sun and the moon.

Netherlands   The flag of the Netherlands derives from the colours of William of Orange who led the independence movement in the sixteenth century. The top stripe was originally orange, forming a flag called the *Prinsvlag*, but became red about 1650. The jack also dates back to those critical years, being based on the flag used by the States-General. The royal standard has the Dutch lion in the centre, and the bugles of Orange-Nassau in the cantons. The standard of Prince Claus is blue with an orange cross, and has a Dutch lion in the first and fourth quarters and a white castle in the others. All the royal standards employ the traditional blue, white and orange colours.

All eleven provinces of the Netherlands have their own arms and flags, as do most of the cities and communes.

Netherlands Antilles   The flag is based on that of the Netherlands, and dates from 2 December 1959. At that time the blue band contained six white stars to stand for the six Dutch dependencies in the West Indies, but on 20 March 1986 the stars were reduced to five, following the promotion of

258   Niger: national flag

259   Nigeria: national flag

260   Norway: national flag and civil ensign

261   Norway: royal standard

262 Oman: national flag

263 Pakistan: national flag

264 Pakistan: President

265 Azad Kashmir

Aruba to self-governing status. **Aruba** has a flag adopted in 1976. **Bonaire** has a flag adopted in 1981. The flag of **Curaçao** was adopted in 1984. **Saba**: The island flag was the winning design in a competition and was adopted on 6 December 1985. **St Maarten**: The flag was introduced on 13 June 1985, and contains the whole arms adopted on 17 November 1982. Only the island of St Eustatius is now without a flag.

New Zealand New Zealand became independent in 1917, but kept the flag adopted in 1869. This is very similar to that of Australia, but has only four stars of the Southern Cross, and these are red with white borders. The civil ensign is red with white stars and the naval ensign white with red stars. The royal flag is a banner of the arms with the royal cypher in the centre. The Air Force ensign is that of the UK (see p. 36) with the letters NZ in the centre of the roundel. The civil air ensign is also like that of the UK (p. 37), with the red stars, edged white, in the lower fly canton.

Cook Islands These are a self-governing dependency of New Zealand. A new version for local use was introduced in August 1979. It has a ring of fifteen stars, one for each island.

Niue The flag of Niue, also a self-governing dependency, was adopted in October 1975. The bright yellow field stands for the warmth of friendship between Niue and New Zealand.

Nicaragua The national flag is identical to that of the United Provinces of Central America of 1823–39, to which Nicaragua once belonged. The national arms which appear in the centre of the State flag and ensign are very similar to those of the United Provinces. The present form of the flags dates from 1908.

Niger The orange disc in the centre represents the sun, the orange stripe the Sahara desert, and the green stripe the grasslands, divided by the white river. This flag was adopted in November 1959, prior to independence in 1960.

Nigeria The green in the flag of Nigeria represents the green land of the country, and the white is for peace. The flag was adopted on independence in October 1960. The naval ensign is like that of the UK but with the flag of Nigeria in the canton.

Norway The flag of Norway was first adopted in 1821, but was not brought into general use until 1898. It is derived from that of Denmark, to which Norway once belonged. The naval ensign is swallow-tailed with a tongue, one of the few of this shape still in use. The royal standard is a banner of the arms, which show the ancient lion of Norway grasping the axe of St Olav. The Crown Prince's is the same, but swallow-tailed.

Oman For several centuries Oman used a plain red flag, but in December 1970 a new range of flags was introduced, using the state emblem in the canton. The national flag also adds white and green panels to the original red. The emblem is a native dagger crossed by two sabres and three links of a chain. The Sultan's standard is red with a green frame in the centre, containing the national emblem ensigned with the royal crown, all in gold. The naval ensign is blue with the national flag in the canton and a white upright foul anchor in the fly.

Pakistan Like that of India, the flag of Pakistan is based on that of the principal independence movement, in this case the Moslem League. The white vertical strip was added on independence in August 1947 to represent non-Moslems. The civil ensign is red with the national flag in the canton. The naval ensign is like the national flag, but has the ratio 1:2 rather than 2:3. The President's flag is like the national flag but with his emblem in the green panel in gold (a crescent and star within a wreath and the name 'Pakistan' in Urdu). This was introduced in this form in 1973.

Azad Kashmir is that part of Kashmir occupied by Pakistan. The orange panel on its flag stands for the Hindu population, next to the emblem of the Moslem League.

Panama Based on that of the USA the flag of Panama was adopted in December 1903, when the country broke away

266 Panama: national flag and civil and naval ensign

267 Papua New Guinea: national flag

268 Paraguay: national flag and civil and naval ensign—obverse

269 Peru: national flag and civil ensign

270 Philippines: national flag

271 Philippines: President

272 Poland: national flag

273 Portugal: national flag and civil and naval ensign

from Colombia. The colours are said to represent the Liberals and the Conservatives. The flag is also used in the Panama Canal Zone.

267 **Papua New Guinea**   The flag of Papua New Guinea was adopted in March 1971, prior to independence in September 1975. It was designed by a local art teacher, and combines the traditional emblem of New Guinea, the bird of paradise, with the Southern Cross of Australia.

Paraguay: national arms   *Paraguay: Treasury Seal*

268 **Paraguay**   Paraguay is one of the few countries to have a national flag with a different design on each side. The difference lies in the central emblems, as shown. The obverse has the national arms in the centre, and the reverse the Treasury Seal. The present design of the national flag dates from 1842, but is based on earlier designs going back to 1812. The President's flag is blue, with the state emblem (without the title), in the centre, and a gold star in each canton. The jack is a square white flag with a gold star (known as the 'Star of May') in the centre of a saltire of red and blue arms.

269 **Peru**   The red and white colours of Peru date back to 1820 when José de San Martin liberated the country. Flags with various designs in these colours were used until 1825 when the present design was adopted. The President's flag is white with the whole national arms in the centre, and a gold Inca sun in each canton. The naval ensign is like the national flag, with a

Peru: whole arms   *Peru: simplified arms*

simplified version of the national arms in the centre. The jack is white and square, with a red border all round and the simplified arms in the centre.

Philippines The Philippine flag was adopted during the struggle for independence against the Spanish in the 1890s. The flag was made official in 1919, and was adopted as that of the independent republic in July 1946. The colours are probably derived from those of the USA. The three small stars stand for the three main island groups. The sun is the 'Sun of Liberty', and its eight rays stand for the eight provinces where the rebellion began.

The President's flag is blue with the state badge in the centre, within a ring of fifty-one stars. The jack is blue with the sun and stars as in the national flag.

Poland The colours of the Polish flag are derived from the ancient arms, a white eagle on red, which date from at least 1241. The flag was re-established as the national flag in 1918 and has remained in use ever since. The arms, in which the eagle was deprived of his crown in the Communist period, appear in the centre of the white strip to form the state flag and civil ensign. The naval ensign is like this but swallow-tailed. The President's flag is a banner of the arms, and previously had an

274 Qatar: national flag

275 Romania: national flag and civil and naval ensign

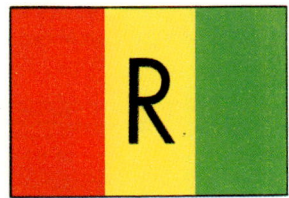

276 Rwanda: national flag

277 St Kitts-Nevis

278 St Lucia: national flag

279 St Vincent and the Grenadines: national flag

280 San Marino: State flag

281 São Tomé and Principe: national flag

282 Sa'udi Arabia: national flag—obverse

283 Senegal: national flag

ornate white frame around the edge, but it is not certain if this is still in use. The Jack is square, white over red, with a counterchanged cross pattée charged with a red disc containing a mailed arm and sword, a design based on earlier military flags.

273 **Portugal** The central device on the flag of Portugal has remained unchanged for centuries: the white shield with five smaller shields (the *quinas*) and a red border with seven gold castles. The *quinas* reputedly date back to 1139. The 'Bordure of Castile' was added in 1252, and the armillary sphere in 1815. The latter represents Portugal's rôle in early voyages of discovery. The colours were adopted in the revolution of 1910: they were previously blue and white. The President's flag is green with the emblem from the national flag in the centre. The jack is a red field with a green border, and is charged with the same emblem.

Qatar Originally the flag of Qatar was ordinary red, but sun and sea turned it to the present maroon colour, which is now
274 official. The flag, dating back to about 1855, was retained when the country became independent in September 1971.

Romania Blue, yellow, and red are colours of the provinces which came together to form Romania in the nineteenth century. Until the events of December 1989 the national arms appeared in the centre. Originally those of the kingdom, they
275 were replaced by a Communist emblem in 1948. The flag also serves as a civil and naval ensign. All the Communist designs have been suppressed since the overthrow of the Ceaućescu regime, but to date no new emblem has been devised to go in the centre of the flag.

276 **Rwanda** The letter R on the flag of Rwanda was added when the country became independent in July 1962, to distinguish it

from that of Guinea. The colours are the Pan-African colours, chosen by the dominant political party.

Saint Kitts-Nevis These islands became independent on 19 September 1983 with a new flag and coat of arms. The flag was the winning entry in a local competition. The two stars do not stand for the two islands but for hope and liberty. The previous flag, adopted 27 February 1967, represented the three islands of St Kitts-Nevis-Anguilla, but Anguilla having seceded from the group remains a separate British dependency (see page 44).

St Lucia This island became independent of the United Kingdom on 22 February 1979, but the only change made to the flag adopted in March 1967 was to alter the proportions. Originally the flag was 5:8 but its shape is now 1:2. The central emblem can be interpreted as the volcanic peaks of the Pitons rising from the golden sands amid the blue sea.

St Vincent and the Grenadines These islands became independent on 27 November 1979 with a flag of vertical blue, yellow, and green vertical stripes containing the whole coat of arms on a stylised breadfruit leaf in the centre, and with white borders to the yellow strip. However, on 21 October 1985 a new version of the flag was introduced. This omits the white fimbriation, and replaces the coat of arms and leaf with three green diamonds, expressive of the state's nickname: 'the Gem of the Antilles'.

San Marino Possibly the oldest state in Europe with a continuous history of independence, San Marino has a flag in colours derived from its arms, which portray three towers on a blue field. The general flag is plain, but the State flag has the arms over all in the centre.

São Tomé and Principe The two stars stand for the two islands, on a flag in the Pan-African colours. Before independence

284 Seychelles: national flag

285 Sierra Leone: national flag

286 Singapore: national flag

287 Solomon Islands: national flag

288 Somalia: national flag

289 South Africa:
national flag and civil ensign

290 Transkei

291 Bophuthatswana

292 Ciskei

293 Venda

147

in July 1975 the liberation movement used the same flag but with stripes of equal width.

282 **Sa'udi Arabia** The inscription on the flag of Sa'udi Arabia is the *shahada*, the Moslem statement of faith: 'There is no God but Allah, and Mohammed is the Prophet of Allah.' The green is the colour of the Wahabi sect. This is the only national flag where the charge on the reverse side is not a mirror-image of the obverse. This is achieved by sewing two copies of the flag together. The royal flag is the same design, but has the national emblem in gold in the lower fly canton.

283 **Senegal** The green star on the flag of Senegal distinguishes it from that of Mali, a country to which Senegal was joined when they achieved independence in 1960. The flag then had a black ideogram called the *kanaga* in the centre, but when Senegal seceded in August of that year this emblem was replaced by the green star, taken from Senegal's coat of arms.

Seychelles These islands became independent in June 1976, but altered their flag just one year later, following a bloodless
284 coup d'état. The present national flag is based on that of the currently dominant political party. The President's flag is the same design but has a white disc in the centre bearing the coat of arms.

285 **Sierra Leone** The flag was adopted on independence in April 1961, and employs colours found in the coat of arms.

Singapore Red and white are colours often used in south-east Asia, and the flag of Singapore is only distinguished from
286 that of Indonesia by the crescent and stars. The flag was originally adopted when Singapore was a crown colony, in 1959, and was retained when it seceded from Malaysia in August 1965. The civil ensign is all red with the crescent and stars within a ring, all in white in the centre. The President's

Singapore: civil ensign

flag is red with the crescent and stars in large proportions. The naval ensign is white with the President's flag in the canton and a red and white compass rose in the fly.

Solomon Islands   These islands became independent in July 1978 and adopted a flag granted the previous November. The colours are said to represent the green land, the sun and the rivers. The five stars stand for the five districts. The flag of the Governor-General is unusual in that the title is written on an outline frigate bird instead of the usual scroll (see p. 73). The Solomon Islands have a full range of ensigns: the civil ensign is red with the national flag in the canton. There is also a new coat of arms.

Somalia   This flag was adopted in October 1954, when Somalia was under United Nations aegis, and the colours and general design are based on the UN flag. The five points of the star are said to stand for the five areas where Somalis live. The flag was retained on independence in July 1960.

South Africa   It is no coincidence that the flags of South Africa are like those of the Netherlands, since they have a common origin in the *Prinsvlag* (see p. 133). The national flag dates from May 1928, and is intended to represent the English

South Africa: President

294 Spain: modern state flag

295 Sri Lanka: national flag

296 Sri Lanka: President's flag

297 Sudan: national flag

298 Surinam: national flag and civil ensign

299 Swaziland: national flag

300 Sweden: national flag and civil ensign

301 Switzerland: national flag

302 Syria: national flag

and Afrikaner elements in the population. The small flags in the centre are the Union Jack, for the two British colonies of the Cape and Natal, and the flags of the former Boer republics of the Orange Free State (in the centre) and the Transvaal. The *Prinsvlag*, or 'Van Riebeeck Flag' as it is known in South Africa, was chosen to commemorate the colonization of South Africa by the Dutch in the early seventeenth century under Jan van Riebeeck. This design became the civil ensign and jack in 1951 and was retained when South Africa became a republic in May 1961. A new flag for the State President was adopted on 14 September 1984, consisting of the national colours arranged to form a white triangle based on the hoist. In its centre is the national coat of arms with the letters S.P. above it. The previous flag was blue with the arms and initials in the centre. The naval ensign is white with a green Scandinavian cross, and the national flag, fimbriated white, in the canton.

The flags of the Orange Free State and of the Transvaal are still in use, and there are also flags for the 'homelands' established for the African population. Four of these are regarded as independent by South Africa: **Bophuthatswana** (1977), **Ciskei** (1981), **Transkei** (1976), and **Venda** (1979). Their flags were all adopted prior to independence (dates in brackets).

Spain The basic form of the national flag of Spain dates from 1785, but the current pattern was only established at the end of the civil war in 1939, although it had been used on the Nationalist side since August 1936. The republican flag, used 1931–9, had three equal horizontal stripes of red, yellow, and purple. These colours are derived from the arms of Castile and León, which may be seen as the two upper quarters in the jack. The two lower quarters in the jack are for Aragon and Navarre.

The coat of arms, which appears on the state and government flags, dates in its present form from December 1981, although the quarters are all of ancient origin. They represent the ancient

Spain: arms

Spain: royal standard

kingdoms of Castile, León, Aragon, Navarre, and Granada. The shield also contains the badge of the house of Bourbon (three gold fleurs de lis on a blue oval) and is supported by the Pillars of Hercules.

The Royal Standard was adopted in April 1971 and has the shield supported by the 'saltire raguly' of Burgundy and the chain of the Order of the Golden Fleece. This is all in full colour on a blue field.

All the modern regions of Spain have their own arms and flags. Amongst the best known are those of the **Basque Lands** (red with a green saltire surmounted by a white cross), **Catalonia** (nine horizontal stripes of yellow and red), **Andalusia** (a horizontal triband of green and white), and the **Canary Islands** (a vertical tricolour of white, blue, yellow).

Sri Lanka The core of the flag of Sri Lanka is the dark red field with the lion and sword. This is based on the flag of Kandy, the central kingdom of Ceylon. This flag was adopted on the independence of Ceylon in February 1948. In 1951 the orange and green panels were added, representing the Tamil and Moslem minority groups. In May 1972 the country became a republic, and the devices in the cantons were altered to represent the leaves of the *bo* tree. The national arms were also altered at

303   Tanzania: national flag

304   Thailand: national flag and civil ensign

305   Togo: national flag

306   Tonga: national flag and civil ensign

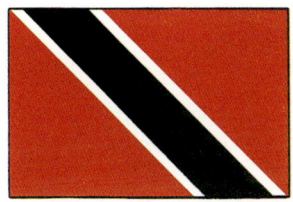

307   Trinidad and Tobago: national flag

308   Tunisia: national flag

309   Turkey: national flag

310   Tuvalu: national flag

this time, and a flag was introduced for the President. This was altered in 1989 to the present design in which the central element is a stylised lotus-flower. The *bo* leaves also appear in its corners.

The civil ensign is red with the national flag in the canton. The naval ensign is like that of the UK (see p. 36), with the Sri Lanka flag in the canton.

Sudan The colours of the flag of the Sudan are those common to most Arab countries, although a variety of meanings are attributed to them. The present design was adopted in May 1970, and replaced the first national flag, which was horizontally blue, yellow, and green, and which had been adopted on independence in January 1956. The President's flag is like the national flag but with the arms in the centre of the white stripe.

Surinam Surinam became independent in November 1975 and adopted a flag based on those of the main political parties. The coat of arms has remained basically the same as that introduced in December 1959. The arms are added on a square white panel, replacing the star on the national flag, to form the President's flag.

Swaziland The flag of Swaziland was adopted on independence in October 1967. It is based on that of the Swazi Pioneer Corps which served in the British Army in the Second World War. The shield etc. date back to 1890 when the country was previously independent. The staff and shield bear tassels of widowbird and lourie feathers, an ornamentation reserved for the King. The shield is that of the Emasotsha regiment.

The royal standard is the same as the national flag, but has a small gold lion in the top blue stripe, facing the fly; this dates from September 1968.

Sweden The colours of Sweden are derived from the national arms: three gold crowns on blue. The flag dates from the mid-sixteenth century. The special 'Scandinavian' form of the flag

Sweden: Greater State Arms

dates from 1665, and it is similar to that used in neighbouring countries. The distinctive form of the naval ensign, swallow-tailed with a tongue, is also particularly Scandinavian.

The royal standard is like the naval ensign, with a white panel in the centre of the cross charged with the whole arms, known as the Greater State Arms. Other members of the royal family have a similar flag, but charged with the Lesser State Arms. There is also a royal pennant of blue over yellow, with the Greater Arms on a white field in the chief. This can be used in conjunction with either of the standards.

The jack is the same as the ensign. The flag of the Minister of Defence is square, divided vertically blue and yellow. On the blue are three crowns, and on the yellow a blue upright sword. The Supreme Commander has a square flag divided blue over yellow horizontally. On the blue are the three crowns, and on the yellow two crossed blue and gold batons. The King's personal flag is a square banner of the royal arms.

The flag of **Scania** (*Skåne*) in southern Sweden is like the national flag, but yellow on red.

Switzerland Although Switzerland is an old country its flag is of comparatively recent adoption. The white 'couped' cross is an old emblem, originally that of Schwyz, one of the three original cantons. The flag was adopted in 1848. The civil ensign, known since 1911, was adopted in 1941 for use on the Rhine.

311   Uganda: national flag

312   United Arab Emirates: national flag

313   USSR: national flag

314   USSR: naval ensign

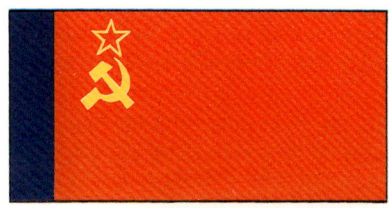
315 Russian SFSR

316
Armenian SSR

317 Azerbaidzhan
SSR

318 Byelorussian
SSR

It is like the national flag but with the ratio 2:3 as opposed to 1:1. Every city, commune, and canton of Switzerland has its own arms and flag. The flags are usually square banners of the arms.

Syria Syria joined the Federation of Arab Republics in January 1972, and adopted the common flag referred to under Egypt (p. 100). However, in April 1980 she reverted to the flag used prior to the Federation, which has two green stars on the central white band. The national emblem has also been altered.

Taiwan See China p. 92.

Tanzania Tanzania is an amalgamation of Tanganyika and Zanzibar, formed in April 1964. The flag of Tanganyika was originally green, black, green, horizontally, with yellow fimbriation, and dated from independence in December 1961. The present design includes a blue portion representing Zanzibar. This is taken from the blue, black, and green flag of Zanzibar.

Thailand The traditional emblem of Thailand is a white elephant on red, which provides two of the colours of the *Trairanga*, or tricolour, as the national flag is called. The blue was added in 1917 to symbolize solidarity with Allies. The white elephant, in caparisoned form, still appears in the centre of the naval ensign.

Syria: national emblem

The royal standard is charged with the *Garuda* in red on royal yellow. The *Garuda* is a mythical bird which features in Buddhist and Hindu mythology, and also appears in the arms of Indonesia. The flag of a royal prince is a blue square with the *Garuda* on a yellow disc in the centre.

The jack is like the national flag but has the naval emblem over all in the centre in yellow. This consists of an anchor passing through a *chakra* and ensigned by a Siamese helmet. The *chakra* is cognate with the one in the flag of India (see p. 117). The flag of an Admiral of the Fleet is a blue square with five white *chakras* around a device of crossed artillery shells and a wreath. Lesser admirals have only the *chakras*, in number according to their rank. Thailand has a very wide range of flags for the services and government departments.

Togo The colours of Togo are the Pan-African colours first used by Ghana (p. 112). This flag was adopted on independence in April 1960 but was inspired by one used under the French administration.

Tonga The flag of Tonga is the same now as it was when the islands became a British Protectorate. It was adopted in 1875, with the proviso that it should never be altered, and it was retained when the country regained its independence in June 1970. It signifies the Methodist persuasion of the inhabitants. There is a royal standard, also dating from 1875. This is a banner of the royal arms.

Trinidad and Tobago The flag was adopted on independence in August 1962. The civil ensign has the ratio 1:2 and the national flag the ratio 3:5. The colours are taken from the coat of arms. The royal flag, used until the country became a republic in October 1976, was a banner of the arms with Queen Elizabeth's cypher in the centre. The naval ensign is like that of the UK (p. 36) but with the national flag, fimbriated white, in the canton.

319 Estonian SSR

320 Georgian SSR

321 Kazakh SSR

322 Kirghiz SSR

323 Latvian SSR

324 Lithuanian SSR

325 Moldavian SSR

326 Tadzhik SSR

308 **Tunisia** The flag of Tunisia was adopted in 1835, prior to the French occupation, and was retained on independence in March 1956. Tunisia became a republic in July 1957, and the Bey's standard became obsolete. The crescent and star and the red and white colours are taken from the flag of Turkey, to which Tunisia once belonged.

309 **Turkey** The crescent and star on the flag of Turkey have been explained in many different ways, none very satisfactory. The crescent has appeared on Turkish flags for many centuries, but the star was only added in the early nineteenth century. The flag was regularized towards the end of the last century, and was retained when the Ottoman Empire became the Republic of Turkey in October 1923.

The President's flag is a square version of the national flag with a gold device in the upper hoist.

Tuvalu Formerly the Ellice Islands, Tuvalu was established as a separate British colony in October 1975, and became independent on 1 October 1978. The flag adopted on inde-
310 pendence has a light blue field with nine gold stars scattered over the fly, representing the nine islands of the group. In the canton is the Union Jack. There is also a coat of arms, granted in 1976, which appeared on the previous Blue Ensign.

311 **Uganda** The emblem in the centre of the flag of Uganda is the African Balearic Crane, which was formerly the ensign-badge. It was also the badge of the dominant political party at the time of independence in October 1962. The colours too are those of the then dominant party.

The President's flag is red with the colours in narrow stripes along the lower edge, and the whole arms in the centre.

United Arab Emirates The colours of the UAE are those
312 common to most Arab countries. The flag was adopted on independence in December 1971. Each of the seven members

has its own arms and flag. The flags of the various emirates are all red and white, originating in the treaty of 1820.

Union of Soviet Socialist Republics The red flag appeared again in the revolution of 1917, having been used by revolutionaries on several previous occasions. It is said to have its origin in the Red Flag used by the Paris mob in the French Revolution. The red star was used by the Bolsheviks and by the Red Army, and so found a place in the new national flag in November 1923, along with the hammer and sickle representing industrial and agricultural workers. The basic design of the flag has remained unchanged since 1923, but regulations of 1980 permit the omission of the hammer, sickle, and star from the reverse side. This is also true of the flags of the constituent republics.

The jack of the Soviet Navy is red, with the red star fimbriated white and charged with the hammer and sickle. The naval ensign is white with a light blue strip along the lower edge, and the red star and the hammer and sickle in large proportions on the white field.

The Soviet Union is a federation of fifteen constituent republics, each with its own arms and flag. The largest republic, and the core of the Soviet Union, is the Russian Soviet Federal Socialist Republic. Its flag is like that of the USSR but with a blue vertical strip in the hoist. This was adopted in January 1954, replacing the original Soviet Russian flag. Each autonomous republic also had its own arms and flag, but these are only variations of the emblems of the RSFSR itself.

Following the introduction of *perestroika* and *glasnost* the individual republics have taken more powers for themselves. Many have declared their sovereignty, and in the case of Lithuania their independence. As a result the Soviet flags are being replaced by pre-Communist ones. The ones most frequently seen are: **Estonia**, horizontally blue, black, white: **Latvia**, dark red with a horizontal white stripe: **Lithuania**,

313

314

315

319
323
324

327 Turkmen SSR

328 Ukraine SSR

329 Uzbek SSR

330 Uruguay: national flag and civil and naval ensign

331 Uruguay: jack

332 Vanuatu: national flag

333 Vatican City State

334 Venezuela: national flag and civil ensign

328 horizontally yellow, green, red; **Ukraine**, blue over yellow:
320 **Georgia**, dark red with a canton of black over white:
316
317 **Armenia**, red over blue over orange, and **Azerbaijan**, blue over red over green with a white crescent and star over all near the hoist. In the case of Russia the flag is the pre-Revolutionary tricolour of white, blue and red.

330 **Uruguay**   The 'Sun of May' on the flag of Uruguay is like that on the flag of Argentina, to which country Uruguay once belonged. Independence was achieved in July 1828, and a flag of nineteen blue and white stripes was then adopted. These were
331 reduced to nine in July 1830. The jack is the flag of José Artigas, dating from April 1815, when he made the first attempt to free Uruguay from foreign rule.

The President's flag is white with the whole arms in the centre.

332 **Vanuatu**   The former New Hebrides, previously ruled jointly by Britain and France, became independent under this name in July 1980. The new national flag is in the colours of the dominant political party, and includes a well-known local emblem, a boar's tusk, containing two crossed fern leaves, symbolic of the traditional way of life. The flag of the President is green with a red border all round, and the whole arms in the centre.

333 **Vatican City State**   This flag was formerly the civil ensign of the Papal States, suppressed in 1870, but resurrected in minuscule form in June 1929. The keys are the emblems of St Peter, and the colours of the flag are derived from them.

334 **Venezuela**   The colours of Venezuela are derived from the flag introduced by Francisco de Miranda in 1806 in the first

campaign to free South America from Spain. The seven stars stand for the seven original provinces. The State flag has the national arms in the canton; these were adopted in 1836, after secession from Greater Colombia. The President's flag is a square version of the national flag, with the arms over all in the centre and a white star at the centre of each side.

Vietnam This flag dates from the 1940s, when left-wing nationalists first began to struggle for independence. It became the flag of the state established in September 1945 in the north. The Communists gradually won control of the whole country, the final victory being in April 1975, after which the flag became that of a united Vietnam. 335

Western Samoa The flag was first adopted in 1948, and amended in February 1949, when Western Samoa was under the administration of New Zealand, on behalf of the United Nations. It was retained when the islands became independent in January 1962. The stars are those of the Southern Cross, and the general design recalls early flags of Samoa. 336

Yemen North and South Yemen, formerly the *Yemen Arab Republic* and the *Yemen People's Democratic Republic* united on 22 May 1990 to form a single state. The new arms and flag are more like those of the former North Yemen than those of the South, the flag being exactly the same except for the omission of the central green star. The flag of the former South Yemen had the same red, white, black colours (the "Arab Liberation" colours) but with a blue triangle based on the hoist and charged with a red star. 337 338

Yugoslavia Red, white and blue have been used in Yugoslavia since the colours were first adopted by Serbia in 1804, which borrowed them from the Russian flag. In 1918, when

335 Vietnam: national flag

336 Western Samoa: national flag and civil ensign

337 Yemen: national flag

338 Yemen People's Democratic Republic: national flag

339 Yugoslavia: civil ensign

340 Yugoslavia: President

341 Bosnia-Herzegovina

342 Macedonia

Yugoslavia was formed, they were placed in their present order. In January 1946 the red star, the emblem of Tito's partisans, was placed on the flag. The national flag is long, i.e. in the ratio 1:2, and the civil ensign short (2:3), the reverse of the usual practice.

The President's flag is square, with the national arms in the centre. The arms have six torches, representing the six constituent republics. The date is that of the proclamation of the republic. The naval ensign is red with the national flag in the canton, fimbriated white and with the red star surrounded by a gold wreath.

Each of the constituent republics has its own flag and emblem. The flags are based on those of the pan-Slav movements of the nineteenth century, in most cases with a red star, like the one on the national flag, added over all, although Bosnia-Herzegovina and Macedonia have flags invented in 1946. Montenegro's flag was designed in 1946, and the flag of Serbia in 1947. In 1990 both Croatia and Slovenia dropped the red stars from their flags and in the case of Croatia the ancient shield of white and red checks was restored.

Zaire The present design was adopted in November 1971, and is the third national flag since the then Belgian Congo became independent in June 1960. It is based on the flag of the governing party, which shows a hand grasping a torch. It is also in the Pan-African colours.

Zambia The flag of Zambia was adopted on independence in October 1964. The colours are based on those of the ruling party, although in an unusual and striking design. The President's flag is orange with the whole arms in the centre. The orange in the flags represents copper, the country's main mineral resource.

Zimbabwe The legal independence of what was once Rhodesia was achieved on 18 April 1980, after a brief return to British rule. The country is named after an ancient African city where the 'Zimbabwe Bird' was found. This featured on previous flags, and is now placed on the red star of socialism in the hoist of the new flag. This is striped in the colours of the ruling Zimbabwe African National Union. The Zimbabwe Bird and the red star are also the crest of the new coat of arms, and form a sort of national badge.

The President's Standard is green with the whole arms in the centre. In the hoist is a white triangle containing the red star and Zimbabwe bird, and in each fly canton are stripes of red, yellow, black, yellow, red—the ZANU colours.

343 Montenegro and Serbia

344 Croatia

345 Slovenia

346 Zaire: national flag

347 Zambia: national flag

348 Zimbabwe: national flag

349 United Nations

350 International Red Cross

351 Olympic Games

INTERNATIONAL FLAGS

There are a large number of flags used internationally, on a world-wide scale, by inter-governmental organizations, defensive and economic alliances, religious groups, political and cultural movements, and other bodies of all kinds and purposes. The following is a very short selection of the many that could be presented.

United Nations Outstanding among them all is the flag of the United Nations, officially adopted on 29 October 1947. It is in the colour now known as 'United Nations Blue', and the flag bears the UN emblem in white. This is a map of the world projected from above the North Pole, surrounded by olive branches of peace. The flag is flown all over the world on United Nations Day, 24 October, and in times of conflict by UN forces and observers.

International Red Cross In 1869 in Switzerland, the countries of the Geneva Convention decided to use the flag of Switzerland with the colours reversed, to mark hospitals and medical personnel in time of war. The Red Cross has thereby become the best-known international badge. Equivalent flags have been adopted for Moslem countries (the Red Crescent), Israel (Red Shield of David) and the Soviet Union (Red Cross and Crescent).

Olympic Games Perhaps the best-known of all international flags, this dates from 1913. The original flag, known as the standard, is carried from one Games to another. The five interlaced rings of different colours represent the five continents.

North Atlantic Treaty Organization The NATO flag dates from October 1953. It is a compass rose within a ring and four rays, all in white on a blue ground, representing the Atlantic Ocean.

Europe In 1986 the **European Community** adopted the flag that had been used since 1955 by the **Council of Europe**, thus giving the flag of blue with twelve gold stars a much wider claim to being the "Flag of Europe". The twelve stars do *not* stand for the twelve members of the EC or for the members of the Council of Europe, but are intended to represent symmetry and harmony. The flag is also now used by the **European Movement** and by all bodies trying to promote the idea of European integration. The flag is now being used at sea with the appropriate national flag placed in the canton.

Africa There is a flag for the **Organization of African Unity**, adopted about 1965. This has the badge of the organization in the centre, and colours which are not like those of any member country.

America The best-known international flag in America is the **Flag of the Race**, i.e. the Hispanic race. This shows three crosses like those on medieval Portuguese flags, representing the ships of Columbus, and a setting sun in gold representing the West. This flag is widely flown in Latin America on the Day of the Race, 12 October. It was designed by a Uruguayan in 1932.

Asia There is no distinctively Asian flag, but one very widely used, especially in south and south-east Asia, is the international **Buddhist flag**, even though it is of American origin.

Fédération Internationale des Associations Vexillologiques One of the newest cultural organizations to

352 *North Atlantic Treaty Organization*

353 *The Flag of Europe*

354 *Organization of African Unity*

355 Flag of the Race

356 Buddhist flag

357 Fédération Internationale
des Associations Vexillologiques

357 adopt an international flag is the FIAV. This flag was adopted in September 1967, and represents flag-halyards against the blue sky—the same blue as the UN flag. It is flown every two years at the International Congresses of Vexillology, when flag-enthusiasts from all over the world gather together.

SUGGESTIONS FOR FURTHER READING

Flags of the World, E.M.C. Barraclough and W.G. Crampton, Frederick Warne, 1981
Military Flags of the World 1618–1900, T. Wise, Blandford Press, 1977
Flags of All Nations, HMSO 1990
The World of Flags, W. G. Crampton, Studio Editions, 1990
Flag: An Eyewitness Guide, W. G. Crampton, Dorling Kindersley, 1989
The Complete Guide to Flags, W. G. Crampton, Grisewood and Dempsey, 1989
Flags at Sea, Timothy Wilson, HMSO 1986
Flags of the United States, W. G. Crampton, Gallery Books, 1989

Some flag charts currently available:
Flags of All Nations, Brown Son and Ferguson, Glasgow 1990
Flaggen der Welt, Reinhard Ryborsch, Frankfurt 1989
The World of Flags, John Bartholomew & Son, Edinburgh, 1987

To keep up to date with flag changes and for features and articles on flag research, readers are recommended to subscribe to *Flagmaster,* the quarterly journal of the Flag Institute. Enquiries should be addressed to The Director, The Flag Institute, 10 Vicarage Road, Chester CH2 3HZ, England.

INDEX

Page numbers in **bold type** refer to colour illustrations.

Admiralty flag (UK), *see* Lord High Admiral
Afghanistan **63**, 72
African Unity, Organization of 177, **178**
Air Training Corps (UK) 37
Alabama **38**, 61
Åland Islands **95**, 105
Alaska **38**, 61
Albania **63**, 72
Alberta **78**, 88
Alderney 41
Algeria **63**, 72
American Samoa 65
Andorra **63**, 72
Angola **66**, 72
Anguilla 27, 44
Anne, HRH Princess **15**, 28
Antigua-Barbuda **66**, 72–3
Argentina 12, **66**, 73
Arizona **39**, 61
Arkansas **39**, 61
Armenian SSR **159**, 168
Army ensign (UK) **19**, 36
Aruba **130**, 136
Ascension Island 52
Australia **66–7**, 73, 76
Austria **70**, 76

Azad Kashmir **135**, 137
Azerbaidzhan SSR **162**, 168

Baden-Württemberg 109
Bahamas **70**, 77
Bahrein **70**, 77
Bangladesh **70**, 77
Barbados **71**, 77
Basque Lands (Basques) 16, 153
Bavaria 109
Belgium **71**, 80, 81
Belize 71, 80
Benin **71**, 80–1
Berlin 109
Bermuda 27, 33, 45
Bhutan **74**, 81
Blue Ensign (UK) **18**, 21, 24, 33, 36, 37
Bolivia **74**, 81
Bonaire **130**, 136
Bophuthatswana **147**, 152
Bosnia-Herzegovina **171**, 172
Botswana **74**, 84
Brandenburg 109
Brazil **74**, 84
Bremen 109

183

Bretons, *see* Brittany
British Antarctic Territory 45
British Broadcasting Corporation 22, 37
British Indian Ocean Territory 45
British Columbia 78, 88
British Rail 23, 37
British Virgin Islands 45
Brittany (Bretons) 16
Brunei 74, 84
Buddhist flag 177, **179**
Bulgaria 75, 85
Burkina Faso 75, 85
Burma 75, 85
Burundi 75, 85
Byelorussian SSR **159**

California **39**, 60, 61
Cambodia, *see* Kampuchea
Cameroun 75, **85**, 88
Canada 78, **79**, **82**, **83**, 88–9
Canary Islands 153
Cape Verde Islands **83**, 89
Catalonia 153
Cayman Islands 27, 45, 48
Central Africa **83**, 89
Chad **83**, 89
Charles, HRH Prince **14**, 28
Chile **86**, 89, 92
Chiefs of Staff, Chairman of the Joint (US) **34**, 56
China **86**, 92

Ciskei **147**, 152
Civil Air Ensign (UK) **22**, 37
Coast Guard (UK) **22**, 37
Coast Guard (USA) 57
Colombia 12, **86**, 92–3, 100
Colorado **39**, 61
Columbia, *see* District of Columbia
Comoro **87**, 93
Confederate States of America **38**, 61
Congo **87**, 93
Connecticut **42**, 61
Cook Islands **131**, 136
Cote d'Ivoire, *see* Ivory Coast
Costa Rica **87**, 93
Croatia 172, **174**
Cuba **87**, 93, 96
Curaçao **130**, 136
Cyprus **90**, 96
Cyprus, North 96
Czechoslovakia 12, **90**, 96, 97

Defence, Secretary of, (USA) **34**, 56
Defence Staff, Chief of, (UK) **19**, 33, 36
Delaware **42**, 61
Denmark 9, 12, **90**, 97
District of Columbia **59**, 64
Djibouti **91**, 97
Dominica **91**, 97, 100
Dominican Republic **91**, 100

184

Ecuador 12, **91**, 100
Egypt **94**, 100–1, 125
El Salvador **94**, 101
Elizabeth, HM Queen **11**, 25, 28
Elizabeth, HM The Queen Mother **14**, 28
England 9, **10**, 12, **15**, 25, 29, 40
Equatorial Guinea **94**, 101, 104
Estonian SSR **162**, 165
Ethiopia **94**, 104
Europe, Council of 177, **178**

Falkland Islands **27**, 48
Faroe Islands **90**, 97
Fédération Internationale des Associations Vexillologiques 177, **179**, 180
Fiji **95**, 104
Finland **95**, 105
Flag etiquette 21, 24
Flag Institute 8, 24, 181
Flag terminology 17, 20
Flemish flag 80, 81
Florida **42**, 61
France 9, 12, 25, **95**, 105, 108
French Polynesia **98**, 108

Gabon **98**, 108
Galapagos Islands 100

Gambia, The **98**, 108
Genoa 12
Georgia **42**, 61
Georgian SSR **162**, 168
German Democratic Republic **99**, 108
German Federal Republic 16, **99**, 109, 112
Germany 20, **98**, 108
Ghana 12, **99**, 112
Gibraltar **30**, 48–9
Greece **102**, 112–3
Greenland **90**, 97
Grenada **102**, 113
Guam **62**, 68
Guatemala **102**, 113
Guernsey **26**, 41
Guinea **102**, 113
Guinea-Bissau **103**, 113
Guyana **103**, 113, 116

Haiti 100, **103**, 116
Hamburg 12, 109
Hawaii **42**, 60, 61
Herm 41, 44
Hesse 109
Honduras **103**, 116
Hong Kong 49
Hungary **106**, 116

Iceland **106**, 116
Idaho **43**, 61
Illinois **43**, 61
India **106**–7, 117
Indiana **43**, 64

Indonesia **107**, 117
Iowa **43**, 61
Iran 20, **110**, 117
Iraq **110**, 117
Ireland 25, 32, **110**, 120
Irish Green Flag 16
Isle of Man **23**, 40
Israel 13, 16, **111**, 120, 125
Italy **111**, 120
Ivory Coast **114**, 120

Jamaica **114**, 121
Japan **114**, 121
Jersey **26**, 41
Joint Services flag (UK) 33
Jordan **115**, 121

Kampuchea **115**, 121
Kansas **43**, 61
Kazakh SSR **162**
Kentucky **46**, 61
Kenya **115**, 121, 124
Kirghiz SSR **162**
Kiribati **115**, 124
Korea, People's Democratic Republic **118**, 124
Korea, Republic of **115**, 124
Kuwait **118**, 124

Laos **118**, 124
Latvian SSR **163**, 165
Lebanon **118**, 124
Lesotho **119**, 125
Liberia **119**, 125

Libya 100, **119**, 125
Liechtenstein **119**, 125, 128
Lithuanian SSR **163**, 168
Lord High Admiral **19**, 36
Louisiana **46**, 61
Lower Saxony 109
Luxembourg **119**, 128

Macedonia **171**, 172
Madagascar **122**, 128
Maine **46**, 61
Malawi **122**, 128
Malaysia **122**, 128
Maldive Islands **122**, 129
Mali **123**, 129, 148
Malta **123**, 129
Man, *see* Isle of Man
Manitoba **79**, 88
Margaret, HRH Princess 28, 29
Marshall Islands 65, 68
Maryland **46**, 61
Massachusetts **46**, 61
Mauritania **123**, 129
Mauritius **123**, 129
Mecklenburg 109
Metropolitan Police 9, **10**
Mexico **123**, 132
Michigan **47**, 61
Micronesia **62**, 65
Minnesota **47**, 61
Mississippi **47**, 61
Missouri **47**, 61
Moldavian SSR **163**
Monaco **126**, 132

Mongolia **126**, 132
Montana **50**, 61
Montenegro 172, **174**
Montserrat 49
Morocco **126**, 132
Mozambique **126**, 132

Namibia **126**, 133
National Bus Company (UK) 37
Nauru **127**, 133
Nebraska **50**, 64
Nepal **127**, 133
Netherlands 12, 16, 20, 21, **127**, 133
Netherlands Antilles **130**, 133, 136
Nevada **50**, 61
New Brunswick **79**, 88
New England flag **30**, 53
New Hampshire **50**, 61
New Jersey **50**, 61
New Mexico **51**, 61
New South Wales **67**, 73
New York **51**, 61
New Zealand **130**-1, 136
Newfoundland **79**, 92
Nicaragua **131**, 136
Niger **134**, 136
Nigeria **134**, 136, 137
Niue **131**, 136
Norfolk Island 76
Normandy (Normans) 16, 41

North Atlantic Treaty Organization 177, **178**
North Carolina **51**, 61
North Dakota **51**, 61
North Marianas Islands 65, 68
North Rhine-Westphalia 109, 112
North-West Territories **82**, 89
Northern Ireland **23**, 40
Northern Territory 76
Norway **134**, 137
Nova Scotia **79**, 88

Ocean Weather Ships 37
Ohio **54**, 61
Oklahoma **54**, 61
Olympic Games **175**, 176
Oman **135**, 137
Ontario **79**, 88
Oregon **54**, 61

Pakistan **135**, 137
Palau 65, 68
Palestine, Arab 121
Panama 137–40, **138**
Panama Canal Zone 140
Papua New Guinea **138**, 140
Paraguay **138**, 140
Pennsylvania **54**, 61
Peru **138**, 140–1
Philip, HRH Prince **11**, 28
Philippine Republic **139**, 141

Pitcairn **30,** 52
Poland 20, **139,** 141, 144
Portugal **139,** 144
Prince Edward Island **82,** 89
Puerto Rico **62,** 68

Qatar **142,** 144
Quebec **82,** 89
Queensland **67,** 73

Race, Flag of the 177, **179**
Red Cross, International **175,** 176
Red Ensign (UK) 13, **18,** 21, 24, 32, 33, 44
Rhineland-Palatinate 112
Rhode Island **54,** 61
Romania **142,** 144
Royal Air Force **19, 22,** 36–7
Royal Fleet Auxiliaries 33
Royal Marines 36
Royal Observer Corps 37
Royal Yacht Squadron 33
Russia 12
Russian SFSR **159,** 168
Rwanda **142,** 144–5

Saarland 112
St Andrew, Cross of **15,** 29, 32, 40
St George, Cross of 12, **15,** 29, 32, 40

St Helena 52
St Kitts-Nevis **142,** 145
Saint Lucia **142,** 145
St Vincent **143,** 145
San Marino **143,** 145
São Tomé and Principe **143,** 145–8
Sark 41
Saskatchewan **82,** 89
Saxony 112
Saxony-Anhalt 112
Sa'udi Arabia **143,** 148
Scania (*Skåne*) 157
Schleswig-Holstein 112
Scotland 9, **10,** 12, **15,** 24, 25, 28, 29, 32, 40
Sea Cadet Corps 36
Senegal **143,** 148
Serbia 172, **174**
Seychelles **146,** 148
Sierra Leone **146,** 148
Singapore **146,** 148
Slovenia 172, **174**
Solomon Islands **146,** 149
Somalia **146,** 149
South Africa **147,** 149, 152
South Australia **67,** 76
South Carolina **55,** 64
South Dakota **55,** 64
Spain **150,** 152–3
Sri Lanka **150,** 153, 156
Sudan **150,** 156
Surinam **151,** 156
Swaziland **151,** 156
Sweden **151,** 156–7

Switzerland 16, **151**, 157, 160
Syria 100, **151**, 160

Tadzhik SSR **163**
Taiwan **86**, 92
Tanzania **154**, 160
Tasmania **67**, 73
Tennessee **55**, 64
Texas **55**, 60, 64
Thailand **154**, 160–1
Thuringia 112
Togo **154**, 161
Tonga **154**, 161
Transkei **147**, 152
Trinidad and Tobago **155**, 161
Tristan da Cunha 52
Tunisia **155**, 164
Turkey **155**, 164
Turkmen SSR **166**
Turks and Caicos Islands 52
Tuvalu 124, **155**, 164

Uganda **158**, 164
Ukraine SSR **166**, 168
Union Jack 13, **15**, 16, 17, **18**, 20, 21, 29, 32–3, 36
Union of Soviet Socialist Republics **158**, 165, 168
  flags of republics **159**, **162–3**, 165, **166**, 168
United Arab Emirates **158**, 164–5

United Kingdom 25–44
  countries of **15**, **23**, **26**, 40–1, 44
  defence forces **18**, **19**, **22**, 33, 36–7
  dependencies **26–7**, 30, 44–5, 48–9, 52
  government and national corporations **18**, **22–3**, 37, 40
  national flags **15**, **18**, 29, 32–3
  royal standards **11**, **14–15**, 25, 28–9
United Nations **175**, 176
United States of America 53–69
  Confederate State flags **38**, 60
  defence forces **34–5**, **38**, 56–7, 64–5
  dependencies **62**, 65, 68–9
  government flags **34**, 56
  national flags **30–1**, 53, 56
  state flags **38–9**, **42–3**, **46–7**, **50–1**, **54–5**, **58–9**, 60, 61, 64
Uruguay 12, **166**, 168
Utah **58**, 64
Uzbek SSR **166**

Vanuatu **167**, 168
Vatican City State **167**, 168
Venda **147**, 152

189

Venezuela 12, **167**, 168–9
Venice 12
Vermont **58**, 64
Vexillological Associations, International Federation of, *see* Fédération Internationale des Associations Vexillologiques
Victoria **67**, 76
Vietnam 169, **170**
Virgin Islands of USA **62**, 69
Virginia **58**, 64

Wales 12, **14**, **23**, 24, 25, 28, 40
Wales, Prince of **14**, 25, 28, 29
Wales, Princess of 29
Walloon flag 81
Washington **58**, 64

Washington, George 53, 64
West Virginia **59**, 64
Western Australia **67**, 73
Western Samoa 169, **170**
White Ensign (UK) 13, **18**, 33, 36
Wisconsin **59**, 64
Women's Royal Air Force 37
Wyoming **59**, 64

Yemen 169, **170**
Yemen Arab Republic 169
Yemen People's Democratic Republic 169, **170**
Yugoslavia 12, **171**, 169–72
Yukon **83**, 89

Zaire 172, **174**
Zambia 172, **175**
Zimbabwe, 172–3, **175**